The Ngöndro

PRELIMINARY PRACTICES TO MAHAMUDRA

A COMMENTARY BY

Ringu Tulku Rinpoche

First Published in 2008 by
Bodhicharya Publications
28 Carrick Drive, Coatbridge, Lanarkshire, ML5 1JZ, Scotland
mgtfrd@aol.com
www.bodhicharya.org

First Edition
Printed by the MPG Books Group in the UK

ISBN 978-0-9534489-6-8

Transcribed and edited by Corinne Segers, Brussels, 1996.
Further editing by Maggy Jones, Samye Ling, 1997 -'98.
Further editing by Ringu Tulku, Margaret Ford and Tim Barrow 2008.
Typesetting and design by Paul O'Connor at Judo Design, Ireland.

The Karma Kagyu Refuge Tree, painted by R.D. Salga.
Commisssioned by Karma Jiga for Rokpa Dundee. Photo by Karma Chodron (Robert Bichan Msc).

All other photos: Paul O'Connor

This Ngondro commentary was taken from a series of teachings given by Ringu Tulku in Brussels in 1996. Rinpoche gave the teachings at the request of Samye Dzong Brussels.

We would like to thank the following people who contributed to this publication, including: Corinne Segars, Maggy Jones, Maria Huendorf, Tim Barrow, Peter Ford and Paul O'Connor.

With grateful thanks to Venerable Karma Jiga and Karma Chodrak of Rokpa Dundee Scotland, for the image of the Ngondro Refuge Tree, from an original Thangka by Ringu Tulku's brother Salga.

Our special thanks to Ringu Tulku for giving these teachings and allowing us to make them available to a general audience. Also, for his support and help in producing this booklet.

Margaret Ford
On behalf of Bodhicharya Publications
March 2008

Contents

Introduction

In the olden days, the practitioners of Dharma used to follow a progressive sequence. They would be taught the first level and practise it, then they would be taught the next and practise that, and progressively move on. This used to be the tradition. Nowadays, there are so many books and teachings going on everywhere that you seem to get everything at the same time. There is no longer a progressive sequence, which can sometimes be quite confusing, because we have so many pieces of information and we don't know where to put them. If we knew how to put them in the proper order, there would be no problem, but we don't, and it puzzles us.

Traditionally, you would first gain a basic understanding from very general, introductory teachings and then you would usually come to their practical side, which is Mahamudra[1]. However, Mahamudra does not start with Mahamudra; it starts with the Preliminaries to Mahamudra, which is what we call the Ngöndro Practice.

Almost everybody who wants to practise Mahamudra has to practise Ngöndro beforehand. The Ngöndro practice is one of the main practices in all Vajrayana schools, but this one I am going through is Ngondro to Mahamudra. For those who practise the Kagyu tradition, this is one of the main practices, and is almost a "must".

I do not really know whether "preliminaries" is the right word, because it sometimes gives the wrong impression. The preliminaries are not just something you do in the beginning and then leave behind, but they are the very essence, the real basic foundation of Mahamudra. The more you understand them, the deeper it becomes, and when you get the Mahamudra teachings, when you really practise Mahamudra, you will find out that everything was already there, in the preliminaries.

It is so important to know the basics well. When I was young I wanted to make cars and aeroplanes and people told me that I needed to study mathematics first to learn this. So I bought some small books on geometry and algebra and went to a friend who passed school, to learn from him. When we opened the geometry book, there was a diagram, a triangle with the letters a, b and c at each corner.

"What are these a, b, c?" I asked.
"Well, they are imaginary points" he answered.
"What is an imaginary point?"
"Well, you just have these points, and you call them a, b and c".
"What does 'a' mean?"
"Nothing, it's just an imaginary point."
"And 'b'?"
"Well, just another imaginary point."
"How can 'a' mean nothing, and 'b' just nothing?
 It must mean something, why then 'a'?"
"No, no, it is not necessarily 'a', it could be d, e, f, or z, anything!"

It was completely beyond my understanding, so that was my last class on geometry! I then thought that mathematics was very difficult. Much later, as a grown-up, I taught at the university and there was a mathematics department. I told the professor that I thought mathematics was completely beyond my scope of understanding and he asked me why. I told him the story and explained my problem. Then he said: "No, it is easy. Suppose you are building a house from here to there, the distance is this much, the width and height are that much. Then you make a point here, and here, and there, and you measure it. You know how many bricks you need". So it became very clear. If my first teacher had explained it like that from the beginning, maybe I would now be a mathematician! I think it is like that with everything. If you miss the basics, then you will not know what you are talking about.

It is also true for Dharma practice. Sometimes you do things, but you don't know what you're actually doing. It happens so often, especially Dharma in the West. Actually it may be truer for Tibetans, because we are so used to it. Everything, every word, is so familiar to us that we take it for granted. We have heard it so many times, since we were very small, and since it is so familiar, it seems to be all right, and acceptable. We mumble through the text, and we seem to know the meaning because it's so familiar, but we actually do not know. When you recite something every day, it seems to be all right, but when you really want to know what each word means, it is sometimes quite difficult. However, if you don't understand that, you don't understand anything. Therefore, it is very important to try to understand the elementary things one by one, both through analysis and from an experiential point of view.

Sometimes we talk about very simple, basic things like Shiné[2] meditation, or the four fundamental thoughts and they are not very difficult to understand theoretically, so we think that we know them. But if we don't really go deeply into them, we don't get to the bottom, to our actual experience, so then we miss their actual meaning. When we have the right understanding of the basics, when it is really strong, then all the rest comes naturally. It is true for me and I think it must be the same for others too.

In the beginning, we feel attracted to "big names", like "Mahamudra", "Dzogchen"[3] and things like that. "Wow! I'd like to practise Mahamudra, or Dzogchen, or the Six Yogas ..." Actually, if you don't have the basics, these higher teachings just won't mean anything to you. You can read the books, you can get the teachings, and even all the initiations and empowerments[4], but it will not blossom into your experience. When that happens, you will come to the conclusion that it does not work and you will reject it as useless. In fact, it is not true that it does not work, but because **you** lack the real basics, you have not really understood the real way how to practise.

This disparagement of very valuable teachings is a big problem. I have seen it in different places. Once a Lama promised to teach Dzogchen somewhere, but he didn't, he taught something else. All the students were complaining, so I told them of my own experience. Since I have this name of a "Tulku"[5], I have received every teaching from everybody. That's the good or the bad thing about being a tulku; the lamas consider that you have been practising for many lifetimes, so they give you all the teachings. However, after having received all these teachings from beginning to end, I felt the need to go backwards. The more teachings I have received, the more I have gone backward in my actual practice. Not forward, but back, back to the beginning! I think this means you have to begin with the beginning. Maybe it is particular to me, I don't know, but I think it is valid for everybody. Maybe you can go backwards as I did, but it may be easier to start from the beginning.

It is very important to understand the basic things. If you have a doubt, if something is confusing, try to clear it, otherwise whatever you build on it will be based on a misunderstanding, on a wrongly preconceived idea. This often happens.

More fundamental is to make sure why we are practising Dharma. We talk about practising different kinds of things, like Mahamudra, but the basic question is why are we doing all that, why should we practise Dharma? If we are not clear about what we are doing, then we are just wasting time. So why are you practising Dharma?

(Different answers from the audience):
- *To try to become kinder to other people.*
- *To come to know better my inner landscape and live more and more in clarity and light instead of confusion.*
- *To progressively get more and more out of my own sufferings and to help others to get rid of their own problems.*
- *To find out what is genuine in ourselves and make it grow.*
- *To live in the present moment and not beside it.*

You are all saying more or less the same thing; it's about getting rid of suffering and becoming more happy and finding ways to help others become happy too. But in order to do that, why practise Dharma? Is there no other way?

- *We have met Lamas who give us the impression that they have reached that goal or are on the right way. It seems to be a valid model to follow.*

Maybe you have too much faith in the Lamas!

- *There has been proof that it works.*
- *This tradition goes so far back, it has been twisted all ways, but still it keeps its purity and efficiency.*

How do you know?

- *I speak from experience. Well, my experience is very limited of course, but I experience it and it works!*

Maybe your experience is different from that of other people. How can you trust your experience, as it always changes? What do you understand by Dharma?

- *We have read the story of the Buddha, it's a nice story, we want to believe it, to follow it.*
- *It is what shows us the nature of mind.*

Yes. That is the main thing. The Dharma is not just a nice story. If it was just a nice story, it would not mean much. Of course it is mainly to find a lasting peace and happiness, but that involves firstly seeing the truth. What we mean by practising Dharma is that we are trying to understand and find the truth, to see the way things really are. Practising Dharma is important because it means we try to find our real self, our true nature, what we really are, to learn how to really be ourselves. When we talk about the "true nature", sometimes it is very much misunderstood, and many times when I hear people talking about seeing their true nature it sounds just like jargon.

When we say we try to see our true nature, it immediately implies that at this moment, we are not seeing our true nature. It means that we are confused. We have lots of doubt and we are not clear. If we do not have a clear understanding and a clear vision, if we are confused and in doubt, that means we are deluded and there is something wrong. Lots of misunderstandings come out of not seeing things clearly. Even in our daily life a misunderstanding can lead to grievous mistakes and wrong judgements.

Once we accept that we do not see things clearly and completely, we must find out whether there is a way to see them clearly and completely. For as long as we do not, we shall be unable to escape out of confusion. Moreover, when we are not clear, when we harbour lots of doubts and confusion, we are unable to make others understand how things really are because we do not understand it ourselves. We cannot guide somebody else when we are blind ourselves. Therefore we should first clear our own vision. When our vision, our understanding is clear, only then only will we be able to guide others.

The most basic and most fundamental procedure in Buddhism, and maybe in all spiritual paths, is to understand ourselves completely, and to clear our own confusion and misunderstandings. Then we can see clearly what we and all phenomena are. If we see it, we see the truth.

All our problems arise out of confusion, out of misunderstandings, wrong assumptions, wrong concepts and ways of seeing things. That is the main Buddhist theory. That is why ignorance is pinpointed as the basic problem in all Buddhist teachings. Out of ignorance come all the other problems. When we say "ignorance", it does not mean that we are lacking a Ph.D. Degree, that we are lacking information about everything. It means that we are not clear basically and all our presumptions and assumptions, all our concepts are built on that confusion.

When you make a foundation of sand bricks without cement, whatever you build on top of it will collapse. The real reason why we should practise Dharma is to clear away this misunderstanding and try to see things clearly. But then, it is not just about information. If I just tell you: "It is like this!", and you say: "Oh, yes!" It won't work, that is too easy. Our confusion has built up over a very long time, and is very deeply ingrained. We have become so habituated to certain ways of thinking and behaving, and through analysis we may come to accept that it is not the way, but still this is not enough. It's not only information and analysis that we need, but transformation at a very deep level of consciousness. This is what Dharma practice is, it's nothing more than seeing things clearly and getting out of confusion. This is why we need many different methods at different stages, in order to deal with our ingrained habits. Then we are mainly dealing with the mind. Sometimes we have problems defining what mind is. It may be understood as the thinking mind, the thoughts. Here what I mean by "mind" is rather the whole of consciousness. That is the "thing" we are dealing with, because that's what we are, and mind is the more important element in a person.

I think it is also very important, when we talk about practising Dharma, to emphasise that, at least from the Buddhist point of view, it is not something that you do as an extra in addition to your usual activities. It is something you find you must do in order to be whole. It is something that if you do not do it, then you feel you are not complete, you are not fulfilling your own purpose, your own objectives and aims. It is for your own well-being, your own good and the good of others, something vital that you cannot do without. When you understand it in that way, you do not practise Dharma because you are in trouble, or because you have nothing else to do: you practise it because it is almost a means of survival, like food and water. If you understand it properly, there is not one circumstance in life when Dharma practice is not necessary. Here, Dharma practice is not only the particular practices like Ngöndro, or Mahamudra, or meditation.

Meditation may be Dharma practice, or it may not be Dharma practice. Ngöndro is not necessarily Dharma practice, and any practice is not necessarily Dharma practice. Doing nothing is not necessarily not practising! That is why we can say that there is no such thing as a non-practising Buddhist. There may be non-practising Christians, who do not go to Church, but there are no non-practising Buddhists!

The real Dharma practice, if you understand it as a totality, starts with very basic things. From the Buddhist point of view, anything you try to do towards what we call "enlightenment" or realising the truth is Dharma practice.

Therefore, when the Buddha taught, he gave teachings at many different levels. He taught different people different things according to what they were able to understand and practise. This is why there are all those different kinds of teachings that were later categorised in, for instance, the Three Yanas. The purpose of this multiplicity of teachings is to show that the practice of Dharma is not just one thing, but many different things at many different levels. For instance, at the basic level[6], what is taught is to work at the level not of our mind, but of our actions, and to try to refrain from doing things that will bring bad results for ourselves and for others. If you do something that brings a negative result and you try to understand what are the causes that generate suffering and pain, and refrain from doing those things, that is Dharma practice.

This approach is not particularly spiritual. It's just very practical and rational. It is ordinary common sense. Then you go further and you try to do something that will bring a good result, for you and others. You try to find out what brings us good results, what stops us from generating negative results, and then we try to do that actively. That is also Dharma practice, maybe a slightly superior form of Dharma practice.

Now that you are actually doing something, you find out that while you are performing these actions with your body or with your speech, it is basically your mind that generates these actions. In order to do anything, we can only use our body; our speech or our mind, there is no other way. This is the usual Buddhist way of categorising. Do we have anything else apart from body, speech and mind with which we can do anything? It's all we have. Out of these three ways or mediums of expression, mind is the most important, because it directs the other two. You can't do anything without the mind first giving orders. If you want to do something nice, like for instance giving some sweets, first your mind has to decide: "I'm going to be very nice and give this to him." If you want to be very nasty also, and even before your body acts, the expression on your face indicates your intention.

Mind is like a chief giving orders, although the action and the result, the effect, is accomplished with body or speech. If your body is doing something positive or negative, if your mouth is saying something positive or negative, it has actually originated in your mind. Therefore, the mind is the main protagonist. From the Buddhist point of view, mind is the most important constituent of a person. If we have to change, to improve, to develop something in ourselves, to change some of our ways, we can only do this through changing our mind. We will only succeed through transforming or improving our mind. We will not change by any other means.

In Dharma practice the mind is the target, the subject, the main material, we could say the raw material, on which we work. Dharma practice is almost nothing else than working on our mind, and by so doing, we work on our whole being. All our suffering, all our happiness, all our emotions come from our mind. Practising Dharma is nothing but dealing with our mind, working on it in many different ways, at many different levels.

When we talk of meditation, it means trying to make our mind a little calmer and clearer. If we try to change our attitude, the way we see things, the way we react, that is also working with our mind. When we try to become kinder, more loving, more compassionate, when we try to develop our positive side, that is again working with our mind. When we try to control and reduce our negative emotions, like anger, jealousy and so on, it is still working with our mind. Mahamudra is nothing different.

Since Dharma practice is working with our mind, dealing with our mind, studying our mind, therefore Buddhism is very individualistic, very personal. It is not a social practice. What I mean by this is that I can work with my mind. I cannot work with somebody else's mind. As I deal with my own mind, I practise on my own, but it does not mean that it has no effect on others. Basically, I have to work with my mind first, but with the intention of helping others. When I improve myself, when I become clearer, more realised, more "enlightened" in a way, then I can also benefit and help others. On the contrary, if I am completely confused myself, I cannot really help anybody else. Of course, if I have the good intention of trying to help others, it is very good and I should try to do whatever I can. Trying to do something for others at a practical, more social level is also practising Dharma, and it is very important. But since our main problem is the way our mind functions, we should focus mainly on working on our mind.

Whether you suffer or whether you are free from suffering depends on how your mind functions, on how it reacts. For instance, even if I have enough to eat, enough to wear, a place to stay and no problems, I can still be very unhappy, or I could also be very happy, depending on my mind. Also, even if my body is not that well, I could still be fine in my mind, I could even be happy. Maybe you have seen such people who are dying, who are very sick, but who are still very happy. That is due to the way their mind functions, the way they see things.

If we can work with our mind, so as to find peace and the correct way of seeing things, then we will have no problems. We shall feel like this, not only when everything is going the way we want, but even when everything goes wrong with us, we shall not be completely down or depressed. That is the main purpose of dharma practice. Therefore, when we are working with our mind, we are actually working with our whole experience.

When we try to understand Dharma, to understand the teachings, it is not enough to believe that if the Buddha said it, it must be the truth. Of course it must be true if the Buddha said it, because he is Buddha. But for us, that is not enough, because when we encounter problems, just remembering what the

Buddha said might help a little, but not really. We have to understand out of our own experience and this is why it is not just information that we need, but real contemplation. For instance, the Buddha said "Everything is impermanent". We may think, "Oh, yes, everything is impermanent, of course!" But when something really happens to us, when we are struck by impermanence in our daily life, then we panic, we become desperate and completely frustrated. If our understanding remains superficial we will not really benefit too much from it.

However, if we understand that everything is impermanent from deep down within our own experience, at our heart level, then when impermanence manifests itself clearly, we do not have a negative reaction. We do not feel that bad, because we knew that it could happen any time. That is the difference between an intellectual understanding and an experiential understanding of Dharma.

When we talk from the point of view of the Ngöndro, or the point of view of contemplation, it means that we actually try to bring all this knowledge at the level of our experience. We could say we try to understand it really, quite deeply, from the bottom of our heart. Then it actually helps, we are really working with our mind. In that case, even the smallest, the tiniest Dharma practice will have a real result, a real impact, because it comes from your experience. Otherwise, just studying everything from beginning to end, and just intellectually knowing everything about the whole Buddhist Canon, the whole Buddhist philosophy, does not really mean too much. You can recite the whole Kangyur[7] and Tengyur[8], but of what help will it be? This is illustrated by a story from the Buddha's life.

One of the Buddha's assistants had been serving him for a long time, and he had heard a lot of teachings, which he knew by heart and was very proud. Once he got a little annoyed, and he left the Buddha. Wherever he went, he used to tell people that: "Except for a kind of radiance emanating from his face and body, the Buddha is not different from me. I know whatever he knows." He actually knew all the teachings by heart, but it did not help him. It did not benefit him because he had not practised anything and his life did not end very nicely.

In the same way, since the main purpose of practising Dharma is working with our mind, if we do not do it, we will not benefit from it. When I talk about practice, I do not mean this practice or that practice, this practice being better than that practice and so on, that's not it. Actually, all practices are the same; all are as good as long as you can work with them on your mind. All the practices are just means, tools to work on your mind. Therefore, if you can work with part of a practice, with one practice, or with all practices, then it is a practice. If you cannot, then nothing is practice. I believe that we can practise many different things together on ourselves. We can practise Mahamudra, Dzogchen, Zen, Mahayana and Theravada together. We can do it because they are all aimed at the same objective; it's just working with our mind. Whatever gives a result, whatever makes us understand and makes us clearer, is working with our mind, and that is practice.

Patrul Rinpoché[9] used to say that if a person gives you a piece of advice, a clue that really helps you work on your mind, even if that person has a hundred faults himself, a hundred negativities, we should take his words as a teaching from the Lord Buddha. We should do this because what matters is that it helps you work on your mind, not where the advice comes from.

In this perspective, even different religions do not matter. As long as it works that way, it does not really matter whether it comes from the Bible, or from Kangyur, or the Upanishads[10] or whatever. It does not matter because you are not working on Kangyur, the Bible or the Upanishads, you are working on yourself. When we talk about the Ngöndro practices, there are sometimes lots of things which people do not understand very well, with which they cannot connect. However, these are all means of training our mind, of working with our mind in different ways.

Our mind is like the yak's horns, very rigid. You cannot bend it because it is rigid and twisted, not flexible. Our mind goes its own way, and because we have become accustomed to that, it is not easy to work with it and change it to the way we would like it to be. This is why we need to use many different methods, different ways in order to tame it, we could say, to make it softer, more pliable. We need very skilful means, because our mind is very delicate.

If you try to force your mind to do something it does not want to do, that is not productive and it can give the opposite result. Working with our mind is a delicate matter and you have to do it in a very skilful and subtle way. The whole practice of Dharma is doing just that.

Questions

In Trungpa Rinpoché's centres, students are advised to practise Shamatha meditation intensively before starting the Ngöndro practices; whereas in other centres like Samyé Ling, students start with Ngöndro and practise Shamatha afterwards. Are both approaches valid or is one better than the other?

Shamatha is a means to make your mind calm and clear, Ngöndro is also that, and both actually work the same way. It does not really matter that much which you practise first, you can also do them simultaneously.

The point is that when you are working with your mind, you need some kind of stability, some clarity of mind, and whichever way you achieve it, that is the practice. You cannot say this is better than that. Actually, to generalise anything is not right. If you say "You **must** first practise Shamatha and then Ngöndro" all the time, it's not right, because maybe that is good for some people but not for others. And if you say "You must **not** practise Shamatha before you practise Ngöndro", that is not right either!

In Tibet we have this saying: "Each Lama has his own religion and each village its own language". Maybe Samyé Ling has its own ways, and Trungpa Rinpoché has his own ways, as everybody has. **You** can have your own way. This does not mean that you completely go out of the system, but how you practise depends on your own experience.

A good teacher does not say, "You have to do this!" He will ask you whether it is all right for you. When I received teachings from Dilgo Khyentsé Rinpoché[11], he would give a teaching from Mahamudra, then give a teaching from Dzogchen and ask me: "Which one do you think is better suited for you?" I would answer, "It doesn't make any difference. It's the same, nothing works for me!"

<hr>

Notes:

1. Mahamudra (chak gya chen po / phyag rgya chen po) : literally "the great seal", the most direct practice for realizing one's Buddha nature, the nature of one's mind. Highest teaching of (mainly) the Kagyu School.
2. Shiné (zhi gnas) : or Shamatha in Sanskrit, is the meditation of calm-abiding.
3. Dzogchen or Dzogpa Chenpo (rdzogs chen) : literally "the Great Perfection" Highest teachings of the Inner Tantra of the Nyingma School of Tibetan Buddhism. Equivalent to Ati Yoga.
4. Initiation/Empowerment (wang / dbang) : ritual conferring the power or the authorization to practice a specific Vajrayana teaching, it is an indispensable door to any Tantric practice. To be complete, the transmission of the text (lung/ lung) and the explanations (tri/ khrid) should also be received.
5. Tulku someone recognized as the rebirth of a previous master.
6. Hinayana : All the Buddhist teachings are subdivided in 3 "yanas" or vehicles :
   1. Hinayana (small vehicle) or Theravada (vehicles of the Ancients - more in favour nowadays to avoid the slightly pejorative connotation of "Hinayana") claims the greatest authenticity, to be closest to the initial teachings of the Buddha. It's ideal is the Arhat, who has reached complete personal liberation.
   2. Mahayana (great vehicle) accepts all the Hinayana teachings, to which it adds the various prajnaparamita sutras. The Mahayana ideal is the Bodhisattva, who works not only for his own but for all beings' complete liberation and enlightenment.
   3. Vajrayana accepts all Hinayana and Mahayana teachings, and adds to them specific techniques aimed for those with the highest capacities (compassion and intelligence) to reach swiftly perfect enlightenment.
7. Kangyur (bka' 'gyur) : Instructions and Precepts of the Buddha, title of a great collection of the Buddha's teachings, translated mostly from Sanskrit into Tibetan, consisting of 108 volumes.
8. Tengyur (bstan 'gyur) : Collection of commentaries on the Buddha's teachings in 225 volumes, mainly translated from Sanskrit and Chinese.
9. Patrul Rinpoché (1808 - 1887) : one of the most outstanding masters of the 19th century.
10. Upanishad : texts on which the Vedanta is based.
11. Dilgo Khyentsé Rinpoché (1910 - 1991 AD) outstanding master of this century and lineage holder of the Nyingma School of Tibetan Buddhism.

The Four Foundations

So far, I have been presenting the introduction to the preliminaries, now for the actual Ngondro.

I have explained that Dharma practice means dealing with our mind, working with our mind, transforming our mind. But why do we need to transform our mind? It's because of our confusion, misconceptions and misunderstandings. We do not really understand who we are.

When our mind is unclear we do not recognise ourselves. In such a situation, many problems arise, we become dissatisfied and we suffer. Therefore, if we can see things a little better; if we can be a little clearer about ourselves and about the things around us, then it will help us to become more aware of the way things really are.

That is why the Ngöndro practice begins with the Four Foundations, or the Contemplations, according to the different translations. With the Ngöndro, we are talking about how we should actually do this practise and how to really experience it.

There is a great deal of difference, as I already explained, but this must be very strongly emphasised, between understanding something and putting it into actual practice. When we talk about contemplation, understanding, analysis and rationalising, we usually get the idea that it is just about logics, we think in a logical way, and come to a logical conclusion and that's the end. From a Buddhist point of view, that is **not** the end that is **not** the real understanding. The real understanding is the experience. There is a great difference between talking about something that you know all about, but that you have not seen, and something you have actually seen. A learned professor who has studied everything about Lhasa and never been there, and somebody who has actually been there, will talk differently about Lhasa. In the same way, if we come to a conclusion through our logical, rational analysis, and if we come to a conclusion through our experience, these two will have many differences.

Therefore, what we need to do here is not just leave this understanding at an intellectual level, but bring it deep into ourselves so that it becomes a real experience. That is what we mean by contemplation, or meditation, whatever you call it. These are the foundations.

The meaning of the foundations is to bring the understanding deep within us, to become part of us. When that happens, then it really works, it makes a difference, and it changes something. Our fundamental outlook, our basic way of seeing things changes so that all the other things, our beliefs, and ways of reacting also change, because these are dependent on our outlook. If we don't change our basic way of seeing things, then the other things won't change either and we will continue to react in the same way as we used to before. We may have some information about how things really are, but that doesn't really matter much, because it doesn't change us and we still function in the same way. When it becomes our experience, then we are transformed.

These four basic thoughts are very simple, but very strong and effective if we can really understand them. They are the Precious Human Life, Impermanence, Karma and Samsara.

1. The Precious Human Life

The practice of Ngöndro ends with the Guru Yoga, and most of the time we are actually doing Guru Yoga. Firstly we feel that our guru, or the lineage of the guru, is in front of us. Then we start our practice with the fundamental thoughts. We recite the lines that are meant to remind us of them. Of course, what is important is to remember them. As I said before, to understand something is fundamental, but once we have understood, the only way to transform this understanding into a deep understanding, into our way of seeing things, is to think about it again and again. We need to be more and more aware of it, to familiarise ourselves with that understanding, to get so strongly habituated to it that it becomes our natural way of seeing things. There is no other way. When we do that, it becomes part of our experience. And this is how the practice is done.

In the actual Ngöndro text, there are just two lines to remind ourselves of the Precious Human life:

> *The first meditation topic concerns the precious human life endowed with every freedom and assets. It is difficult to get and can be easily destroyed, so now is the time to make it meaningful.*

The English translation doesn't sound very poetic, but that's what it means. You can find the definition of what is meant by 'the precious human body' in "The Torch of Certainty¹" and in other books. Sometimes people explain that the human body is not necessarily precious, it is only considered precious when you have a combination of certain conditions. However, all human life is precious, because if you have a human life, you can make it precious. Whether you make it precious or not is very much under your own control.

Most of the time, we don't value our lives as human beings. When we don't value something very much, we don't appreciate it in the right way. When we don't realise the true value of something, we can't enjoy and use it properly. It is only when you know the preciousness of something, when you know that what you have is really valuable, that you can use it according to that value.

Suppose you have a crystal glass, but you don't know it is crystal, then you just use it for everything and maybe you break it. If you know it is a crystal glass, very precious, then you will take care of it and even if you only drink water in it, you will feel very proud and happy because you may be drinking water, but in a crystal glass !

Therefore, the first thing we have to do is to appreciate what we have. If we don't, what's the use of having it? I was so shocked the first time I came to England. A professor came to see me and told me he was going to commit suicide. I asked why and he told me that it was because, for the second time, he had not been allowed to attend a seven days conference in America! I was completely shocked, but he actually meant it, he was very serious. He was a Professor who had prestige, a position, everything, and he made lots of money. But just because his department had not authorised him to go to America he was thinking about committing suicide. How little he valued his life!
If you know how precious your life is, then you won't waste it by becoming sad and depressed or worrying too much about small things.

Therefore, when you know that your life is important, valuable and precious, that it is not something you should waste, you will appreciate it more and use it more purposefully. You won't waste it by making yourself uselessly miserable. If something goes wrong, then all right, it goes wrong, but you still have your life, which is very precious. If you understand this deeply, then even if you have nothing else, completely nothing but just your life, you should still be very happy. Even if you have only a very little time left, you will not panic and waste that little time in unnecessary things, but you will use it purposefully. As you all know, human beings are considered the most intelligent species on earth and we can use this intellect, we can use this power, in a right or wrong way. We can use it to destroy ourselves and the whole universe, or we can use it to benefit ourselves and others. To understand deeply the preciousness of our human life means to understand the great opportunity we have, and we can do so many things, so many good things for ourselves and for others. If we really want to and if we really try, we can even eliminate all our problems. When we develop that understanding, whatever we do is influenced by it, therefore we can't do anything negative, anything really bad, because we know that would be wasting our time.

Moreover, this does not only change our way of looking at ourselves but our way of looking at others. When we appreciate ourselves, when we value our own life, then we value others also. Only when we value ourselves and our own life can we value others. When that changes, we have made a complete transformation. If I appreciate myself as I am, I will not waste my life, and if I appreciate others also, I will not want to waste their time either. If I really see things that way, I have become a very nice person, a good human being. Through meditating, truly contemplating and understanding this first foundation, the Precious Human Body, we can actually transform ourselves and become better people.

Once we have understood the preciousness of human life, we should also realise that it is not easy to get, and that it is very easy to lose. When you understand it deeply, you will feel a strong inspiration, and a strong urge to make something purposeful out of your life. When you know that it is valuable, very delicate and not easy to get, you can use your life very purposefully, and you will make something good of it for yourself and for others. If you really have that understanding it means you have accomplished the first foundation.

Questions

I think that the preciousness of human life is very much linked with our own pure true nature. For me this is quite clear, I believe in the purity of our true nature. But often, when I talk with other people, even very clever people, I find it very difficult to make them understand it. They don't believe in that. Is there a way to explain it clearly so that they might accept the notion? I have tried many times different ways, but I don't succeed.

Neither do I! That's why I didn't mention that! But maybe they will understand it slowly. Usually, when we teach, for instance when we teach language to children, we have to do it gradually. For many years, I was writing school books for children and I had many difficulties writing for primary classes, because one has to write in a manner appropriate to the grade. You can't put in a book for the 2nd class what they will only learn in the 4th class. When you write a lesson for the 1st or 2nd class, you have to make sure that you include what they have already learned or are about to learn. So, if we just jump from the basics; that is, from the precious human body to Buddha nature, it becomes difficult to grasp. Maybe if we go step by step, people will find a connection.

When I come into contact with another person who is suffering, it just breaks my heart. What can I do? I mean, it definitely gives me the responsibility to work on my mind, to become a better person myself, but that is what I can do for myself. Now what can I do for that other person who suffers, how can I alleviate his/her sufferings, make it lighter?

You can't help other people completely, that's true. When you understand that you cannot do much for another person, it means that another person cannot do too much for you either. Therefore, for your own good, you must work on yourself. You must transform yourself, and then only can you maybe help others. How much you can help others also depends on how much you have understood how to help yourself, how to deal with your own problems. If you do not know how to deal with your own suffering, how can you help somebody else who is suffering too? If you know how to deal with your own problems, then it is more likely that you will be able to help others.

In these modern times, people seem to prefer teaching rather than learning themselves, but it is very important to learn first of all how to help ourselves. Therefore, it is one more reason to practise, to learn, to experience yourself, in order to have more experience, more understanding, more knowledge and more skill to help others.

2. Impermanence

The second foundation is impermanence. The root text says :

> *Secondly, the universe and everything that lives therein is impermanent,*
> *particularly the lives of beings, who are like water-bubbles. The time of*
> *death is uncertain, and when you die, you will become a corpse. Dharma*
> *will help you at that time, therefore practise it diligently now.*

All of us know that there is nothing really permanent, everybody dies, everything changes, and we can all see the evidence of it everywhere. It's not a secret, it's not difficult to understand. However, when something happens to us, like for instance a vase falls down and breaks into pieces, or my watch stops working, then I am completely upset. I know that my watch is impermanent, that it will stop some day, but when it actually breaks, it's hard for me to accept. Therefore we need to remind ourselves, to be aware of this fact again and again. It is not an understanding that we recollect occasionally when we read books on Buddhism, or when we meditate on impermanence. It should become our basic way of seeing things. That is what we try to do, because if we really understand impermanence, it can actually change our life, change our way of reacting, our character and our personality.

Let's take a simple example: suppose three or four people are staying together as a family or a group of friends or more people working together, like in a centre - and then they fight, sometimes because of very little things. If they really understood impermanence, they wouldn't react like that. Even if we are a family, and we have come together supposedly for a whole life, we don't really know how long this life will last, maybe only until tomorrow, or the day after tomorrow, or next year ... When we know that it is not going to last very long we will try to make the best out of that short time. If we develop that attitude, that it can't be for a very long time, then even if something goes wrong, it won't be so difficult to bear. It doesn't mean that we should not solve whatever the problem is, of course we should solve the problem, but we won't make an issue of it. We will naturally become easier to live with, because we will no longer react with excessive sensitivity to small things. We will no longer be like what a Tibetan saying defines as a "ball of pus".

When you have a wound, and it becomes infected, full of pus, then whatever touches it, even the slightest thing, it is very painful. If you are like that, whatever touches you will always end badly. When you understand impermanence more deeply, you won't take whatever happens so seriously. I don't mean that you don't take anything seriously, that you don't bother about anything, What I mean is that you don't take things so seriously that you make yourself miserable for even the smallest things. Even if somebody says something unpleasant to you, you can think: "All right, he or she said something bad to me, but if I react by answering something bad to him or her, it will hurt him/her and create more problems, so I will try to reason and solve the problem in a more amiable way. I don't have to become completely angry and start fighting. I will work it out slowly."

All our emotions, especially the negative ones, and especially anger, are such that if you can delay your reaction a little bit, they will go away. If you can wait even just a few seconds, the better part of your consciousness may start to function and you will refrain from reacting according to the negative impulse. You will be glad that you resisted the impulse of doing or saying something that you would have regretted afterwards, and it will give you confidence and joy because you were able to deal with the situation in a better way.

If you develop that kind of attitude within your family, you will have a loving and compassionate family because people usually react to how they are treated by others. So, if you are patient and loving then your family, and others, will be the same with you. However, there are always exceptions at both ends. You can compare humanity to a Gauss curve, at one end, you have the best few, they won't change whatever you do, and they will remain very good and nice, all the time. At the other end, you have the worst few; you can't change them either, because they will remain bad whatever you do. These are fortunately the minority, and all the rest, the majority, can be influenced. If I smile you smile back, if I frown, you frown back. It is like the story of the wise shepherd.

There was a wise shepherd who used to sit on a hill looking after his sheep. His village was down the valley. One day a man came and asked him: "What kind of people live down there in that village?" the shepherd asked him: "What kind of people lived in the village you came from?" And the man answered: "They were very nasty people, quarrelsome, inhospitable, very bad people." "Well", replied the shepherd, "the people down there are exactly like that, just the same, horrible, inhospitable and nasty." Later, another man came and asked the same question and again, the shepherd asked him about the people who were living in the village he came from. The man answered: "Oh, they were so nice, friendly, hospitable, really good people." The shepherd told him "Well, the people down there are just the same, very nice, helpful, and hospitable".

Why did he give two completely opposite answers to the same question? What it means is that whether people are nice or not depends on mainly how you are yourself. If you are nice, compassionate, open and generous, then naturally other people will also be kinder. If you are kind to them, why should they not be kind to you? But if you are rather bad, rather harsh, then it is likely that most people will also behave like that with you. Therefore, if you always have the impression that everybody behaves badly towards you, it probably means that there is something wrong with you and you should look to yourself to change.

There is a story from Kashmir. There was a father and his son, and before he died the father gave his son many pieces of advice. However, there were two things which were quite confusing. One was that he should never walk in the sun when he goes to or from his shop (he was a shop keeper), and the second was that he should marry a new wife every day. He had always been an obedient son, very respectful towards his father, so he thought he must do whatever his father had told him and moreover, (besides these two confusing points) all the other instructions his father had left were very good. He was facing a big problem.

At last, after having searched for a long time, a beautiful girl accepted the deal. The ceremony was prepared and he asked her once more whether she was sure to agree to marry him, because the next day, he would divorce and marry someone else. She answered it was all right. The next morning, when he asked her to go, she refused and told him that he had misunderstood his father's instructions. His father didn't mean that he should marry a new girl each day, but that he should treat his wife every day as if they had just married that day. He thought that she was probably right, that this might be true, and they lived together very well for a long time. Then, because his father had told him not to walk in the sun, he was just sitting inside and not going to work and his business was declining. His wife told him that he had misunderstood yet again, and what his father really meant was that he should go to his shop before sunrise and come home only after sunset!

If we really understand impermanence we would treat our wife or husband as if we are newly- weds and give them all our love, because our time together can end at any time.

Sometimes, people think that if we are talking or thinking about impermanence, we become very gloomy, very serious, but actually, it is completely the opposite! If we really understand, if we are convinced of impermanence, we become broader-minded, more open. Everything changes anyway, I will die, and I don't know when that will happen. If I die tomorrow, all the small problems I have today will disappear the moment I'm dead. If I really know that I can die tomorrow, I will consider the problems I have today from a broader perspective. I will not take them so badly because I am prepared for the worst. There is an English saying that says more or less, "Hope for the best, and prepare for the worst, do your utmost."

When you have this strong understanding of impermanence, you are always prepared for the worst therefore small things can be taken in the right way. You won't react too negatively, even if something goes wrong. If things turn out well, then that it is very good too. Your clinging to things is a little softened and loosened, so that you become more spacious, and therefore more joyful: this really happens. The more you understand impermanence, the more generous you become, because you know that things will change and go away. When something bad happens you will not feel devastated and when something good happens you can appreciate it without clinging.

Besides this, understanding impermanence will lead you to an understanding of the true nature of things. It will make you see more clearly the way things really are on a personal, experiential level. Although understanding impermanence is very simple, it can actually lead you to seeing the inter-relatedness, the interdependent nature of things. This is, what we call "Shunyata", or emptiness, which is the basic, essential philosophy of Buddhism. Understanding Shunyata is actually nothing more than the subtlest, most minute understanding of impermanence. If there is impermanence, it means that everything changes. Everything, even when it is there, is changing, and change takes place within relatedness, each thing affecting each other. This is something you can see, you can understand. If you look more deeply, more closely at a flower, you will understand that the flower is made of so many different parts, it is in interrelation not just with one or two things, but almost with the whole universe. It has connections throughout the whole universe. Therefore, it is not a solid, indivisible, independent entity, it is not just one thing, but it is very complicated, complex, completely interdependent and interrelated.

The Buddha once talked about the "net of jewels", and there is a long sutra on this subject. He gave an explanation of the phenomena of the whole universe by comparing them to a net of jewels. He described a net of very big, shiny and beautiful jewels, like diamonds, cut in more than 100,000 facets each, and in each of these, all the others are reflected. The whole universe, the way things are, is like this, each phenomena reflects all the others, has the cause and effects of all the others; all things are interrelated. There is not one thing which is just one, unchanging and independent, not related to something else. The whole process, the whole universe, all phenomena are like dreams, mirages, waves, water.... bubbles. The Buddha gave many different examples like this.

All these different examples mean that things are at the same time there and not there. They are like a dream. When we say this, we should be careful to define it very precisely because: it is **not** a dream, it is **like** a dream. In a dream you see and you experience things very clearly, everything is there, and you can interact and connect with people and things. However, while you are dreaming: is there actually anything there? When you wake up, you realise that there was really nothing there. The way things are, and their nature, is something like that. It is very much there, but at the same time, it is not as much there as we think. In the same way, it is like a mirage.

Impermanence doesn't mean that everything stops. It means that everything changes. Because of impermanence, because of inter-dependence, there is the possibility of change, of growth, of apparent growth and apparent dissolution. Therefore, what we are now will not last. If we are in a problematic situation, if we experience misery, or suffering, if bad things are happening to us, it can change. If we are in a good position, that can change too. If we are in a very difficult situation we could change it ourselves too. That is the main understanding. Life is changing all the time and we can die any time. Therefore, if we want to improve our way of life, our way of seeing things and our mind, we should do it now, because if we don't do it now, we might not get as good an opportunity in the future.

Meditation on impermanence will also inspire you to practice Dharma. You will understand that to run after worldly things alone does not give lasting happiness for yourself nor help others.

Questions

In the prayer we recite at the end of the teachings, we say that we dedicate the merits of our virtuous actions. How would you define a virtuous action? I'm not interested in an academic definition, I would like your own definition.

"Sönam"[2] is the Tibertan word for this and is a very difficult word to translate into English. "Virtue" has been used, but I don't know how close or how far it is from the actual meaning. "Sönam" means the result of a positive deed. A positive deed is any deed which brings a positive result, that means a good happy result that benefits yourself and others, now or in the long run. In a way, it is any action that is not negative or neutral. What is negative is what brings harm and unhappiness, disharmony, discomfort, to me and others, now or in the long run. What doesn't bring any result is a neutral deed. An action that we do with compassion, wisdom, a good heart, love, kindness, the wish to help, wanting to do good for others or ourselves, all these are positive. If I give this teaching, and you come to listen to it, with the intention to benefit ourselves and others, if we have that motivation, then it becomes a positive deed, and when we dedicate it, it has also a positive result. On the other hand, if I do it in a different way, with a different motivation, perhaps because I have nothing else to do, or because I feel very big and important when I sit on a throne and talk to people, then my motivation is not positive, but rather negative.

What is diligence?

Diligence means hard working, but not just that. The real definition of diligence, "tsöndrü"[3], is feeling joyful in doing something positive. We shouldn't work hard with too much resistance, feeling as if it is an obligation. Diligence is finding joy in doing good things.

3. Karma

Karma means actions and reactions, the causes and effects. It is actually the basic understanding of interdependence. The stanza given here is just a reminder. It says:

> *Thirdly, after your death, you will have to experience your own karma,*
> *having no degree of control over what happens.*
> *So give up harmful actions – all your time should be spent in the practice of*
> *virtue. Thinking this way, evaluate your life daily.*

Karma is very important from the Buddhist point of view. It is not just something you believe in, but something you understand. Whether you believe it or not, your understanding of it makes a big difference to how you see things. In a nutshell, karma means that whatever we do results in a reaction. Anything that happens is the continuation of something that went on before. The theory of karma and the theory of interdependence are actually the same. A combination of a number of particular elements will give rise to a particular situation. Another combination will give another situation. It is like chemistry. If you combine hydrogen and oxygen, you get water. This not only applies to all the things that we see, but also to all our actions. We are completely responsible for what will happen to us in the future, as well as for what we are now, because what and how we are is the result of our past actions. The way we are now will continue into the future, therefore if we don't make any major changes, what we will be in the future will be similar to what we are now, with slight differences of course. The karmic process doesn't function as if somebody was recording our actions in a notebook and deciding what we should be given next, whether in this life or the next.

Anything that we do with strong feelings and emotions is incorporated in our mind stream. It becomes our way of thinking and reacting and it reinforces our emotional and thought patterns becoming part of our own personality. Then we find that the same things happen to us again and again. Many people tell me "I have this problem, which comes from an incident when I was a child. This psychological problem I have now comes from a big trauma I experienced in my childhood". This is well-known and accepted nowadays, but how does that happen? It isn't that you did something in your childhood, or something happened, and then it was recorded, written down and now suddenly there is a payback. What happens is, whatever we do, whatever strong reaction we have, becomes part of our being, it matures in us and when certain circumstances come together, that reaction reappears, sometimes with even greater power.

This process not only takes place in the course of one lifetime, but it builds up over many lifetimes. We can see examples of how karma works in this lifetime, and if we place it in the broader, longer perspective of many lifetimes, we will understand more easily how it functions.

Sometimes, when something negative happens to us, we become very disturbed and completely frustrated. We get very upset because we don't have enough understanding of karma. If we understand karma, it will be easier for us to accept what we are going through. Of course, life is not always walking in a rose garden. There is good and bad, sometimes very good things happen, sometimes very bad ones. If we can take those bad things as the result of our own karma, we will not look for something or somebody to blame, and we won't get angry. Usually, we think we do not deserve bad things and we get angry and resentful. We shouldn't. It happens because of our own past and because of something we did ourselves. However, there is no need to blame ourselves either, because it may be as a result of certain circumstances in the past a very long time ago. When something negative happens to us, we have the opportunity to purify our karma. Karma can be changed because karma is inter-relatedness, interdependence.

This is something that is very, very important to understand; karma is something that inevitably has to change. It has no other way but to change, because it is not permanent or independent. Therefore, if we understand karma, when something negative happens to us, we will not lose hope, because we know it is going to change and by our own efforts too. Everything that happens is only temporary, so even if we experience a big obstacle in our life, we should take it as no more than an obstacle, no more than a temporary negative thing which we need to get through, to work with, and to purify. It is a problem in our mind-stream and we should not be afraid but try to solve it with a quieter, more reasonable, less agitated mind. If we can do that, the result is the purification of that obstacle.

Therefore, karma is that if we do something good, with a good intention, then there is a positive result; if we do something bad, something harmful, then there is a negative result. It is not difficult to understand. If I throw a stone in the sky, it will fall down and hit me; and if I throw a flower, it will also fall back on me. Everything is like that. That is the main understanding of karma.

Now what we are trying to do here is to bring that understanding into our own experience. For instance, if I develop strong anger and become full of hate, what will the result be? What will I become? If, instead, I generate love, kindness, compassion, joy, and if I cultivate these long and strong enough, what will I become? If we can understand this then perhaps we can see how Karma works. It is said that there are many opportunities to become realised or become enlightened, after we die, and perhaps you have read the Tibetan Book of the Dead[4]. Of course, there are opportunities, but it is difficult to see them unless we are prepared for them. In this life too, there are countless opportunities to become a millionaire for instance, there is a possibility, but it isn't very likely. In the same way, the opportunities are there after our death, but unless we have prepared and trained ourselves during this life, it will not be so easy at that time to even see the opportunities. What we are now will continue. In this life, we have childhood, youth, old age. Sometimes people think that because they are young, they have all these problems and these crazy ideas, but when they grow older, everything will calm down. I think that is completely wrong. From my years of experience, I didn't change. So if I did not change after all these years, I think I will not change too much for the years to come. If for the first 30 or more years of a life, I act in a way that makes me more nervous, more anxious, that is what I will become. That continues not only in this life but in the next ones, in a long chain.

Of course, we cannot understand how Karma works in every detail, it is too complicated. Nobody has only good or only bad karma, we all have jumbled up karma; and it is like kedgeree, a dish in India where you cook everything together in one pot. It's actually a mixture of everything, mainly rice, but then you add meat, vegetables, anything you can get. It's the easiest thing to cook, and it's delicious. All the bachelors in India eat kedgeree. Our karma is a kedgeree, so you get everything in it.

When we have this strong understanding of karma, of how it works, then the necessity to work on our negative emotions, on our negative way of living and doing things becomes obvious. We know that if we make very strong negative karma, it will get out of hand and be very difficult, if not impossible, to control. If you have depression, even if you know you shouldn't fall in that depression, you can't push it away, because it has now developed to that stage. Maybe if you had known about it and done something to stop it a long time ago, you could have prevented it. However, now that it has developed to that stage, it is very difficult to get out of it.

In the same way, when our negative karma comes to full maturity, it is very difficult to control. Therefore, with that understanding, we will naturally feel it is urgent, high priority, to do what is positive and refrain from doing negative things right from the beginning. It is not that somebody else tells you that you should do this or that, or that things are prohibited by religion, or by some commandment. Sometimes, everywhere, but especially in the West, people take religion that way, like the Ten Commandments in the Bible, and they react by thinking that it's a commandment, and you usually react against it. On the other hand, if you understand karma, you will just do it for your own sake. If I understand that it is for my own good, I will do it. Thus we naturally try to work with our negativities and refrain from doing negative things, because we know they would have painful results for us or for others. If we know clearly that something is not good for us and not good for others, neither in the short term, nor in the long run, then there is no reason to do it. Even if the wish to do it is there, we will be able to work with it more easily. There is a story to illustrate this:

There was a shepherd who was not very intelligent, but who was very tenacious. The shepherd was very impressed by a hermit and he went to ask him for a practice, but as he didn't understand too much, he asked for a very simple one. The hermit told him to have two bags full of pebbles: one with black pebbles, one with white ones. While sitting looking after his sheep, he was told he should watch his thoughts and if a negative thought came in his mind, he would take a black pebble and put it to one side. If a positive thought came in his mind, he would take a white pebble and put it to the other side. He did this, and after a while he saw that the pile of black pebbles was growing high, while the white pile was very small. He was a little worried, and he went back to the hermit asking him what to do. The hermit told him not to worry and just keep doing as he had been doing. After a while, slowly but surely, the two piles became similar, and after some time, the white pile became bigger than the black one.

If we know what is wrong and what is right, and if we are a little mindful or watchful, we will refrain from the negative. We shouldn't be too watchful though because we could not sustain the effort for too long before becoming tired. When we intend to walk a long way, we walk slowly and don't run, knowing there is a long journey ahead. If we started running, we wouldn't get very far. Therefore it is better to be watchful and mindful in a lighter way. We try to understand clearly, through our own experience, the theory and the working of karma. We can't see the past and the future clearly although we can see a little bit of it.

As we say in Tibetan : "To know what you were in the past, just look at yourself now, and to know what you will be in the future, just look at your actions now." When we understand that doing something positive has a positive result, and doing something negative has a negative result, then the only thing we have to do is be a little watchful, do what is positive and refrain from what is negative. That's the whole idea. When that is done, we have become a better person. If you really believe that if you do something harmful you will get a negative result, you cannot possibly become a completely bad person. Not only that, but that experience of karma, that conviction, will necessarily strengthen your positive way of doing things. This is why understanding karma is so fundamental.

Questions

How can we be sure that our actions are positive or negative?

Generally speaking, if an action is harmful to you and to others, that is negative. If it is beneficial to you or to anybody, that is positive. But as you cannot always say with everything you do whether it will have a harmful or beneficial result, you should watch your motivation. When something you do is motivated or inspired by a good heart, love, compassion, joy, wanting to do something good, and wanting to help, then it is positive. If it is inspired or motivated by negative thoughts and emotions, like anger, jealousy or any of the mind poisons, then it is negative.

You said that each time something negative happens to us, we shouldn't react with resentment and anger, but instead see it as an opportunity to purify our bad karma. What would be the right attitude, between anger or resentment, and falling in the other extreme of being overjoyed each time something bad happens to us, because of the possibility to purify our bad karma ?

I don't think you would be too happy anyway if something bad happens! If you are so happy, then nothing bad is really happening. It is a good thing happening. You will have no problem, you will always be happy, because if something good happens, then you will be happy, and if something bad happens, you will think, "Oh!, still better !" Unfortunately, it does not happen like that. For those who experience life in this way, there are no problems, but for most people, when a bad thing happens to them, they feel resentment, which makes things even worse.

Sometimes, people aggravate the problem so much through resentment that even when the problem itself is gone, their anger and their resentment are still there, and they continue to live with such feelings. It is not a solution, it is a wrong way of reacting, but it is quite common. If we understand that what we face is a karmic reaction, and is happening because of many different reasons, then we will at least not create the extra burden of taking things too badly. If we can see the situation more clearly, we won't add more problems on top of the problems that are already there and it will make things lighter.

4. Samsara

If we have no problems at all, if everything is nice and good, then it is all right. There is no need to do anything else. However if it is not the case, we should try to see what the problems are, which are inherent to this way of life, and their causes. These are the things we need to think about. When we look at our life and others' lives, we see that there are many problems and much suffering. The Buddha himself had no problems but he looked into life and saw birth, old age, sickness and death.

How does old age, sickness and death affect us? Can we escape them or not? We all have to die, we all get old and sick, and although we don't want it, we always get or meet what we don't want and don't get what we actually want. These problems always make us suffer. They happen continuously, again and again. Of course, when we have a problem, we solve it, but then we get another. Also, if everybody has to go through old age, sickness and death, if everybody has problems, why does it bother us so much? Why does it make us suffer? When we consider this, we find that the main problem is our way of looking at things, our way of reacting towards things. We are conditioned in such a way that we almost necessarily get into turmoil.

The text of the Ngöndro says:

> One is constantly tormented by the three kinds of sufferings. Therefore, samsaric places, friends, pleasures and possessions are like a party given by an executioner, who will then lead one to the place of execution. Cutting through the snares of attachment, strive for enlightenment with diligence.

If we are reacting with a Samsaric state of mind we suffer from these three kinds of suffering or dissatisfaction.

The first is the suffering of suffering. When we don't get what we want, or we get what we don't want, or when we experience actual pain, or something that really makes us miserable and is very negative, that is what we call the suffering of suffering.

Of course, we would think that nobody likes to suffer, but I have heard that some people do. They say that it's painful, but it's just life. Many people become so attached to their suffering, and identify so much with their suffering that they don't want to let it go. There is a story about someone who had been suffering, burning in hell for a very long time. When his term came to an end and he was released from hell, he turned back to shout to the beings left there: "Please don't let anybody sit in my place!"

We should understand suffering as suffering; we should not see suffering as something nice and then do nothing. We should be able to see things clearly and accept them as they are.

However, I think it is important to understand what we mean by acceptance. It is not a passive attitude by which we just let things happen without reacting, that is not what we mean by acceptance. It means that we see whatever is going on exactly as it is, not colouring it, not hiding it under a carpet, not cheating ourselves by pretending it is something else. It is seeing suffering as it is but then doing what is necessary and appropriate to get out of it. That is the Buddhist approach to suffering.

Also, if we look at it more closely, even when we are not actually suffering, when we have no definite problem, nor actual pain, we still have a fear of change. That is the second type of suffering, the suffering of change. We are all right now, but it is not going to last. It is when we have everything, when everything is fine and we have no problems, but we worry constantly that something might happen and everything might change. This worry and fear is always there at the back of our minds and in our hearts.

The third type of suffering is the suffering inherent to the nature of everything. Everything changes, continuously and completely, nothing remains as it is, even from one moment to the next. Nothing is permanent. When we contemplated impermanence, we saw that everything is compounded, made of many different things put together. Everything is affected by everything else, therefore everything changes so much and so frequently that even my own being is not stable. Everything is a continuous flow and therefore we cannot rely on anything, not even our own existence. We are not comfortable with this.

We cannot get out of these problems because our mind is reacting in a samsaric way. Samsara is, to make it very simple, a state of mind where we have continuous aversion and attachment. We label everything thinking "this is very bad, I should not have it, I am afraid of it." That is aversion, and aversion is, I think, the main ingredient in the suffering of samsara. When we feel aversion for something, we need to escape and to run away from it, but we cannot run away because aversion overpowers our mind. Aversion gives rise to fear, and because of fear, we also develop attachment. Attachment and aversion are like the two sides of a coin. Because of aversion, we have fear, and because of fear, we try to cling to something, thinking it might be what we need to make all our fears go away. However, even if we run after something and are able to grab it, it never gives us complete peace and happiness because the problem lies in the way our mind reacts. Therefore we continuously run after one thing or another.

For example, I may think I need a glass, perhaps a particular beautiful crystal glass. If I get that glass I'll find lasting happiness. Then I do all different kinds of things, I work hard, I hurt others, I undergo many difficulties and problems, and finally, I get hold of the glass. Then I find that nothing has changed. I am still sad, I still have problems and still I'm afraid. I think that maybe I was wrong, and that it is a flower I need and not a glass. So again I run after the flower and undergo many hardships. At last I get the flower, but still nothing has changed. So it goes on and on.....

The aversion and attachment way of reacting is samsara. In such a state of mind where you are always running away from something, or running after something, you cannot have any peace. This is why we talk of the "Wheel of Samsara". When you have a water mill, the water flows day and night, so the mill is turning day and night, it never stops. That's the same as samsara. We have to run all the time without ever resting. We are always trying to avoid something or to get something. This mentality keeps us in a state of constant suffering. We therefore need to look deeply into this, because if we fully understand what samsara is, we will also understand the possibility of getting out of it. If we can get out of it, then we do not have any problems anymore because we no longer feel any aversion towards anything. Whatever happens is all right, it's good and is wonderful. We also don't fear anything and we don't cling to anything either. Attachment is the need to cling to something because we feel we can't do without it, because we would be threatened if we didn't have it.

Sometimes, people ask me whether there is any difference between love and attachment. There is a big difference. Attachment is self-oriented, you are clutching to something just for your own sake. Compassion and love are directed towards others, not towards yourself. When you are feeling genuine compassion, genuine love, it cannot turn into hatred. On the contrary, attachment can turn into hate just like that, in just a second. That is the difference. If we understand the samsaric way of mind very clearly, deeply, then we also understand the possibility to get out of it, and that means we are on the Path, we are actually practising Dharma. The real practice of Dharma comes from knowing what we can do. That is the main lesson we can learn from the contemplation of samsara.

Questions

Is it possible that we also develop attachment towards Dharma, towards our practice of Dharma?

It depends. It is possible that you get attached to Dharma also. As I explained, attachment comes from aversion, The main difference lies in the way you understand things. If you see the problems clearly, if you know that if you do this, that is going to happen, and then you practise what you can call "Dharma" or whatever, and with that understanding, that is the Path, that is good.

On the other hand, if you say "This is **my** Dharma, this is **my** religion, if anybody says something against it, I'm going to fight them," then that is attachment, it is not good and it won't help you.

Gampopa, the chief disciple of Milarepa said that:

> *"Dharma which is not practised as Dharma can lead you to endless sufferings."*

"Dharma" is a word, a concept. You can use it in a very bad way too, it's up to you. It is because Dharma has not always been used in a "Dharmic" way that many people have so much resistance or aversion to religion. Some people reject religion completely, and not only in the West. This is because there have been people who used the name of religion for their own agenda, their own purposes and ego. Dharma, whether you call it religion or spirituality, is a very important part in every human life; therefore it is the easiest thing to use in order to arouse people's emotions and sentiments.

You said that attachment comes from fear, and you also said that attachment and aversion are like the two sides of the same coin. Can we also say that fear comes from attachment, or desire? There are so many things we can be afraid of - accidents, spiders or mice. So can we say that some of our fears come from unconscious desires, desires we cannot consciously accept and that we transform into fears?

Certainly, attachment and aversion are like two sides of a coin, but fear actually comes from aversion. Aversion is more basic, it is not a specific fear, it is a general way of reacting. I think the reason why some people have more fear of spiders than snakes or vice-versa, depends on their personal experiences. Some people fear loneliness. I know someone who cannot walk 100 yards alone. His fear is so strong that he has physical reactions, he perspires and shivers. However, if somebody is with him, he can go anywhere! Of course, it is all in his mind, but still he can't do it alone.

Also, some people fear crowds, they become afraid if there are more than two people. I know a Tibetan lady who cannot see more than one person at a time. She's been staying in her room for more than 10 years. She sees her husband and her daughter, that's all. Nobody else can see her.

What is the best way of dealing with our fears, what would be the best attitude to deal with the fear of the future?

In a way, the whole purpose of the practice of Dharma is to get rid of our fears. The fear of the future is the same as any other fear. If you think too much about the future, how it may be, how it should be, how it may turn out like this or like that, then you develop fear. Maybe the best way would be to be able to be in the present. It isn't easy, of course, but if anything really worries us and makes us fearful and anxious, it is because we think too much and negatively about either the past or the future.

When we feel tension while doing something, it is not just because of what we do in the present, but also all the things we have in our mind related to the past or the future. Therefore, we should learn how to be a little more in the present, because if we really do the right thing in the present moment, then the future is already, more or less, taken care of. In general, the best way is to adopt the attitude I mentioned before:"Do your utmost, hope for the best and prepare for the worst." When you have that attitude, I think you will have less fear for the future. In any situation, if you can do something, then do it. If you can't, just leave it. It helps me to remember the following saying by Shantideva[5] :

"If you can change it, what is there to worry about?
If you can't change it, what's the use of worrying about it?"

———◆———

Notes:

1. The Torch of Certainty by Jamgön Kongtrul, Shambhala, 1977 (reprinted).
2. Sönam (bsod nams)
3. Tsöndrü (brtson 'grus)
4. Bardo Thödol or "Liberation through Hearing in the Intermediate Period after Death" translated by Chögyam Trungpa & Francesca Fremantle, Shambhala Press, reprinted 1992.
5. Shantideva (7th - 8th C.) Famous Indian proponent of the Mâdhyamika school of Mahayana. Nothing much is known for certain as to his biography, except that he was a monk at the University of Nalanda. He is the author of the Bodhichâryâvatâra.

The Four Special
Foundations

In the preliminary practices to Mahamudra, there are four general foundations, followed by the Four Special Foundations, or inner Ngöndro practices. These belong more specifically to the Vajrayana, as they are the specific preliminaries for the particular practice of Mahamudra. These four preliminaries are :

- *Refuge & Bodhicitta*
- *Dorjé Sempa (Purification)*
- *Mandala Offering (Accumulation)*
- *Guru Yoga*

1. Refuge & Bodhicitta

Refuge

In the Ngöndro, we find a practical way of taking Refuge. There are actually two, even three different ways of going for Refuge and they can be understood at different levels.

Taking Refuge means that we need something or somebody to rely on. We have to find a goal, a purpose, an objective, something we can look forward to. We have previously gone through the different aspects of The Four Foundations, like Samsara. We have perhaps come to realise through contemplation that the samsaric way of living, the samsaric state of mind is very painful and full of suffering, but that there is a way to get out of that state. How can we do that? Can we do it easily on our own, or do we need some guidance? Taking Refuge is actually finding a model and a path. There is something that we can attain, become or discover. There is somebody, or something which can actually give us the guidance. That is the outer Refuge.

Buddha, Dharma and Sangha are what we can rely on because they can grant us protection and freedom from the suffering of the samsaric state of mind. In a deeper, more inner way, taking Refuge is to know that we have a chance to find our inner truth, to realise our true nature and that basic state which is not stained by the samsaric state of mind. There is the possibility of eliminating and transforming our mind into an enlightened state of mind, which we call Buddha nature, or our basic goodness, or our enlightened nature. When we understand that we have the potential to discover that true state of mind, which is beyond suffering, beyond our constant running, or our being totally overpowered by either aversion or attachment, then we take Refuge to our true nature that is there within us.

Taking Refuge at the outer level means that we acknowledge there is something we cannot do on our own. Therefore we need the help of somebody or something else. That is the literal meaning of taking Refuge. We acknowledge that we do not have the insight, nor the knowledge to pull ourselves out of the samsaric state of mind. Therefore we go for help to somebody who has been able to get himself out of samsaric suffering, who knows how to do it.

We take Refuge in the Buddha, because he is a person, or a being who was capable of doing just that, he has the understanding, the experience and the realisation. At the first level, when we take Refuge in the Buddha, we see him as a model and a guide, as somebody who has trodden the path and who has accomplished the great task of getting out of the samsaric state of mind. Whatever we want to do, in any field, we cannot get the understanding and realisation from someone who has not understood or realised themselves. Nobody can guide us unless he or she has walked that path. Therefore we take Refuge in the Buddha.

We take Refuge in the Dharma because that is the actual path. The Buddha is the teacher. The Dharma is the experience of the Buddha on his way to the realisation. Dharma is what the Buddha experienced, what he realised. Therefore, if we follow the same way, we will gain the same understanding, the same realisation. Dharma is the guidance that the Buddha left for us. It is the path we can tread.

Dharma is usually defined as having two aspects, the first being the teachings that the Buddha gave, the Kangyur and Tengyur and all the various books. The second is our own experience and that of the people who have trodden that path. That is the real Dharma and not just the teachings, or the written words of the Buddha. It is what we actually experience when we go through the teachings and apply them to ourselves.

Then we take Refuge in the Sangha. The Sangha consists of the beings who have taken the Buddha's teachings into their actual experience.

Why do we need to take Refuge in the Buddha, Dharma and Sangha? It is because if we go for Refuge with the Buddha, we also need the Dharma. The Dharma is the path, and without it, we could not find our way, and without the Sangha, we could not find the Dharma. Therefore we need to take Refuge in all three together, and when we take Refuge in one, we actually take Refuge in them all. Some people might ask why we don't just take Refuge in the Buddha alone, but that is not a correct understanding of taking Refuge. The Buddha should not be seen as an all compassionate, all knowing being that we pray to and beg to save us. That is not the way.

Whenever we say a prayer, we say that we take Refuge in the Buddha, Dharma and Sangha, because it is not enough to take Refuge in the Buddha alone and expect that we will be saved. We have to tread the path, to find the way, to practise ourselves, and then only can we make some progress. The inner way of taking Refuge is to take Refuge with the Buddha within. By this I mean our real journey is to find our own intrinsic nature, our real basic goodness that is Buddha nature. This is our final ultimate aim, in that to take Refuge in the

Buddha is to find our direction, our own way and purpose. We see how we are now, that we are confused and in a samsaric state. We have all these problems because we do not see our true nature, which is the enlightened state. Therefore our aim and objective is to find Buddhahood, and with this strong sense of purpose, this is taking Refuge in the Buddha. The way that the Buddha gave us to achieve that is the Dharma: and the Sangha is the same as explained before.

Then we have Lama, Yidams and Khandros, which is the Vajrayana way of taking Refuge. It's actually in a way the same as Buddha, Dharma and Sangha. Buddha is the guide, the one who has the experience of the path, who gives the teachings; and likewise, it is the Lama who has the experience, who gives the guidance. Therefore, taking Refuge with the Lama is similar to taking Refuge with the Buddha.

In Vajrayana, the "yidam" is the actual practice, the path, the way to bring out your own Buddha nature and enlightenment. Therefore, going Refuge to Yidam is the same as going Refuge to Dharma. The Khandros, or Dakas and Dakinis, are the Sangha, the spiritual community that preserves and protects the Vajrayana teachings.

In general Buddhism we talk of Buddha, Dharma and Sangha, and in Vajrayana, we call them Lama, Yidam and Khandros, but these are the same. When we visualise the Refuge Tree, we have these six : Buddha, Dharma, Sangha, Lama, Yidams and Dakinis and also the protectors. So far we have seen the meaning of Taking Refuge, but in the Ngöndro practice, we do it in a more visual way, we try to create a mandala.

If we just say "I take Refuge in the Buddha, Dharma and Sangha", it is a rather theoretical, academic, intellectual way. If we want to actually take Refuge in the Buddha, Dharma and Sangha, we have to make it more experiential, it has to feel real, as if it were really happening. Therefore, the main thing is to generate our own devotion and to open up our mind so that we will be able to fuse our mind with the minds of the Buddhas. It is to receive the Buddha, Dharma and Sangha in ourselves and to unite ourselves with these principles in an experiential way.

In order to do this, we use skilful means, and we try to create a mandala. We create a tree, as if we were actually doing it, not in a theoretical way, but from people to people. We try to see the Buddha, the Dharma, the Sangha, the Lama and all these things as actually being present, and then we try to merge our own mind with the Buddha's mind. We try to receive the actual "blessing," or mind-stream, or energies of the Buddha, Dharma and Sangha in ourselves, and not just ourselves, but in all sentient beings too.

If we follow the Mahayana or Vajrayana, we try to become a Buddha not only to help ourselves, but also to help all sentient beings. Therefore whatever we do, we do it with a broader, a more compassionate, Bodhisattva attitude. This is why we include all sentient beings in our Refuge visualisation.

Now, it seems that many people have problems with visualisations, especially in the West. When someone tells me this I usually ask them if they are planning a vacation and ask them to describe their plans. Once they tell me about where they plan to go and what they hope to find there, I tell them that is visualisation. If they can see themselves in Barcelona and lying on the beach enjoying the sunshine, then they are creating a visualisation.

So here, we visualise according to the next part of the Ngöndro, which says:

> In the middle of a lake, in front of me, there is a great wish-fulfilling tree.
> It has a main trunk and five branches. At its centre, where the branches leave
> the trunk, my root-guru, in the apparent form of Dorjé Chang (Vajradhara)
> sits on a lion throne, lotus, sun and moon. He is surrounded by all the gurus
> of the "Oral Transmission" (Kagyu Lineage). In front of him are the
> yidams, to his right the Buddhas, behind him the sacred Dharma teachings,
> to his left the Sangha and below his throne are all the male and female
> Dharma-protectors and guardians. Each of these groups is surrounded by an
> ocean of others like them. All our mothers from the past are standing on the
> beautiful green pastures of the banks of the lake. With full concentration,
> we all take Refuge and resolve to reach enlightenment.

That is the visualisation. We visualise the wish-fulfilling tree, and on top of it is Vajradhara, or Dorjé Chang. He is blue in colour, actually who this figure is doesn't really matter that much. The main thing is to feel that this central figure, in whatever form it appears, Vajradhara or whatever, is the mind, the enlightened state, the enlightened heart of your guru. It's not only your guru, but all the enlightened beings. It is their amalgamation in one, because all the enlightened states are one, the same understanding, the same experience. Your guru and all the enlightened beings, the energy of all the enlightened beings, of all the Buddhas and Bodhisattvas is in that central figure. That is the main visualisation.

Then there is the whole lineage through which the Mahamudra teaching is received[1] - because these are the Mahamudra preliminaries - all the beings, the Lamas, the masters through which the Mahamudra was transmitted are on top of the main image. It goes back to the primordial Buddha Vajradhara.

On the four sides, there are the Buddhas to the left, the Bodhisattva and Vinaya[2] Sangha to the right, the Dharma represented by books at the back, and the Yidams, or deities and their mandalas, at the front. All around are Dharma protectors[3] of all kinds. This is the Refuge Tree.

The main thing is the Guru, in whatever form he appears. It is possible that you cannot be very clear about all the others. If you cannot clearly see them, you can feel them and that's the most important thing. What you try to do is to feel that in front of you is the living Buddha, actually alive, living, radiating enlightened energy. The whole mandala, the whole galaxy of enlightened beings is in front of you. With devotion, trust and faith, you, and all the sentient beings around you, go for Refuge to the Buddha, Dharma, Sangha, Lama, Yidam and Khandro. When you think you would like to follow the instructions of the Buddha and would like to become enlightened, that is taking Refuge in the Buddha. If you would like to follow the Path, that is taking Refuge in the Dharma. If you are ready to take advice and guidance from the Sangha, that is taking Refuge with the Sangha. With this understanding you say the Refuge prayer:

*I, and all beings in number as vast as space, take Refuge in our very
kind root Guru, whose very nature is the combination of the body, speech,
mind, qualities and activities of all the Buddhas of the three times and ten
directions. He is our source of the 84,000 dharma teachings and the Lord
of the Realised Sangha*[4].

That is the prayer, and the important thing is that we try to open ourselves and
our minds, because our real intention is to awaken our Buddha-nature. When
we try to open ourselves to taking Refuge, then our Buddha-nature can come
out, it can blossom. As we try to awaken our own Buddha nature, we try to say
the Refuge prayer with devotion.

Devotion is the most suitable state of mind and emotion to open ourselves
completely. It is an emotion which is very pure, very clear, open, awake
and strong. It is not confused, disconnected or disturbed. If we can create
or rekindle our devotion, it is the state of mind which is the most suitable
for meditation. Many masters achieved true realisation through devotion,
because when you feel devotion, your mind is completely open, ripe and ready
for the realisation of your true nature. When you are in a state of devotion,
you cannot be angry, jealous or proud. You are totally without any of those
negative emotions, therefore you are in the right state of mind. Usually, the
real Mahamudra experience, the real insight or realisation, is always said to
come through devotion.

What happens is not that: "I have devotion to my Guru, so my Guru is giving
me the blessing" and then you receive Mahamudra. That's not how it works.
The most fertile ground for the Mahamudra meditation is devotion. Therefore,
we first generate devotion, and then say the prayer above, which is followed by
another Refuge prayer:

We take Refuge in our most kind root Guru and in all the Gurus of the Lineage,
We take Refuge in all the Yidams of all the Mandalas[5],
We take Refuge in the perfectly realised Buddhas who have transcended suffering,
We take Refuge in the noble Dharma,
We take Refuge in the realised Sangha,
We take Refuge in all the Dakas, Dakinis, Dharma protectors and guardians
endowed with wisdom eyes.

Usually, when we take Refuge, we also do prostrations. Prostrations are a physical, mental and symbolic way of working mainly with our pride. When we do prostrations, we submit and humble ourselves, which is a way to work with our ego. We offer reverence to the Refuge Tree. People usually do 100,000 prostrations and sometimes more.

There is a very nice text, it is actually a prayer, written by Sakya Pandita[6] - a very great master of the Sakya Order, which gives the symbolism of prostrations:

Homage to the Guru
Namo manjushriye – jam pel yang la chak tsal lo
Namo sushriye – lek pay pal la chak tsal lo
Namo uttamashriye swaha – chok kyi pal la chak tsal lo

As I prostrate to the Three Jewels[7]
May all the beings be purified of their negative deeds and defilements
As I join my two palms
May the methods and wisdom combine together
As I place my joined palms on my crown
May we reach the Ultimate Realm
As I place my joined palms on my forehead
May all the negative deeds and defilements of body be purified
As I place my joined palms on my throat
May all negative actions and defilements of speech be purified
As I place my joined palms on my heart

May all the negative thoughts and defilements of mind be purified
As I join and separate my two palms
May I work for the benefit of beings with the two Rupa Kayas[8]
As I kneel on the ground
May all the samsaric beings be liberated from the negative lower realms
As I place my two hand and ten fingers on the ground
May we gradually proceed through the ten Bhumis[9] *and five Paths*[10]
As I place my forehead on the ground
May we attain the Eleventh Bhumi[11]
As I bend and stretch my forelimbs
May I work for all beings through the four types of activities[12]
As I stretch and contract all my muscles and nerves
May all the knots on our channels[13] *be freed*
As I bend my spinal cord forward and backward
May we all have our energy channelled through our central channel
As I stand after touching the ground
May we never remain in samsara but be liberated from it
As I prostrate again and again
May we not remain in Nirvana but lead the beings out of samsara

By the power of this prostration we are presently doing,
May we for the moment have good health and prosperity in life
May we be born in Dewachen[14] *when we die*
May we attain the Perfect Enlightenment very quickly.

BODHICITTA

We are now coming to the second half of this practice, which is the generation of Bodhicitta, which you can almost translate as "the enlightened mind", or "the enlightened heart" - *Chang chub*[15] in Tibetan. A more common way of explaining Bodhichitta is that it means compassion, but a very optimistic and inclusive compassion. What is compassion and how do we generate it?

We should first realise that I, as a human being, do not want any unhappiness, anything painful or bad happening to me. In the same way, all beings, not only human beings, share the same wish. Therefore, just as I wish to be happy and have all that's good, I should try to find a way to free myself from my suffering. However, not only that, I should try to help other beings free themselves from their suffering too.

If a person has a genuine, strong and uncontrived motivation to end his own problems and sufferings, and to attain everlasting happiness, and also if there is the intention to help others find everlasting peace and happiness, then that person is what we call, from the Buddhist point of view, a Bodhisattva. A Bodhisattva is somebody who is on his way to becoming an enlightened being, a Buddha. An enlightened being is somebody who has achieved the understanding, the knowledge and the capacity to free himself from his suffering and problems, and to help all other beings do the same.

When we try to develop Bodhicitta we are aspiring to become Bodhisattvas. By taking Refuge, we have chosen as our goal, or our main objective, to become enlightened beings, who are free of all problems and who can help others. In order to achieve that goal, we have to become Bodhisattvas, because that is the way, the path. The whole practice can be described as trying to become Bodhisattvas, trying to generate that intention, that aspiration or mind-stream in ourselves. That is the most important step we can take towards our aim. In order to become a Bodhisattva, we don't need anything else but compassion, which is sometimes called a good heart.

If you have that kind of aspiration, from the Buddhist point of view, you are a Bodhisattva, and it doesn't matter what religion, what class, what kind of people you belong to. It doesn't even matter whether you are a human being or not, if you have that intention, you are a Bodhisattva.

The wish to help not only ourselves but all the others as well is a very magnificent idea. What we usually do is to try to help ourselves only, even if it means harming others. Here we turn the polarity upside down, we want to help ourselves in order to help all others. This is the most beautiful inspiration that can grow, that can develop in our mind-stream.

As explained before, what we become depends on our mind-stream. Therefore, if such an aspiration or motivation develops in our mind-stream, nothing can be negative or become bad, because the negative things that we feel and see are reflections of our own negativity. As we all know, if I am really angry, in a really negative and bad mood, then I will see everything as dark and unpleasant. I will perceive the people around me as being a little angry too, and if somebody looks at me, I will credit him with bad intentions. On the contrary, when I am in a very good mood, I see everything around me as very joyful and pleasant, as if all the flowers were blooming.

Here, to generate Bodhicitta is the main point, and it means mainly to generate compassion as much as possible. Of course it doesn't mean that as soon as we take the Bodhisattva's vows, we become great Bodhisattvas. We don't become Bodhisattvas immediately, but this is the kind of effort we should make. The path of gradually working on ourselves is the one that we should tread. Actually, there is nothing else in Buddhism, and maybe in all religions or spiritual paths. Sometimes people tend to separate religion and spirituality, but in my mind it is the same in essence. When I say "religion", you may imagine the institution, but that's not the image I get in my mind, that's not religion at all to me. To me, religion is the teachings and practices.

The essence of all religions, of all the spiritual practices is unselfishness. If we read the biographies of all the great spiritual, holy beings, the main characteristic of them all is that they were unselfish. We don't call them 'holy' just because they were learned, as not all holy beings were educated, some of them were not even literate. We don't call them 'holy' because they were famous and powerful, or because they had many followers, as most of them were actually persecuted and killed. The only common criteria, the common characteristic of all holy beings is that they were unselfish.

Now we will look at how we take the Bodhisattva's vows and commitments and how we generate motivation in a concrete way.

We try to generate a strong wish for ourselves and all other beings to become completely enlightened and reach a state of everlasting happiness, and with that motivation, we take the Bodhisattva's vows in front of the Refuge Tree, which is like an energy field of all the enlightened, holy beings. We visualise all the realised, spiritual beings, the masters, all the lineage of great beings, all the Buddhas and Bodhisattvas, all the realised Sangha and the Dharma protectors. We imagine that we and all the sentient beings around us are sitting in front of them, and we all take the Bodhisattva's vows. But firstly we take Refuge once again with the following prayer:

> Until we reach the very heart of enlightenment, we take Refuge in the Buddhas,
> likewise we take Refuge in the Dharma and in the Bodhisattva Sangha.

Having called upon them to witness our aspiration and decision in this way, we then take the actual Bodhisattva's vows:

> Just as the Buddhas of the past first resolved to reach enlightenment and then
> progressed stage by stage through the different levels of Bodhisattva training,
> In the same way, we also develop a mind intent upon enlightenment for the
> sake of all beings and we will progressively practice in that training.

These are the actual words you say, and you try to feel their meaning. With this motivation, this aspiration of kind-heartedness, of compassion, the Bodhisattvas of the past were able to attain great enlightenment and become fully awakened beings who developed compassion and wisdom to their utmost. Having generated the intention to become Bodhisattvas, they didn't become highly attained the next day, or soon after, it didn't happen like that. They habituated themselves slowly but progressively to become Bodhisattvas.

According to the Buddhist point of view, everything is a question of habits. If we feel angry, negative, unhappy, depressed, nervous and stressed, it is because we are habituated to it. If we nurture such a mind-stream, we will feel more and more like that, it is nothing but a bad habit. It is also true for a positive attitude. If we foster joy, happiness, compassion and loving kindness more and more, it will also become part of our way of life. Therefore, whether we want to tread the path of joy, kind-heartedness and compassion, or to follow the one of anger, depression and stress, it is just a matter of choosing one's way and developing those feelings again and again.

In Tibetan, we say "There's absolutely nothing which doesn't become easier by becoming used to it, by doing it over and over again." It's not just a Tibetan saying actually, I'm sure we can find such a saying everywhere. Therefore, the practice consists in doing more and more whatever you want to, slowly developing whatever you want to develop, that is compassion, joy, and the more positive side of yourself.

Sometimes, people think that to become a Bodhisattva means they should become completely unselfish, feel complete love for all sentient beings. They think that it is too difficult, that they can't become Bodhisattvas, and they drop the idea altogether.

It's just a question of effort. If you think that this is a good way, you try to go in that direction and to progress step by step. Step by step means that maybe in the beginning, you don't want to feel too much hatred, because hatred doesn't make you feel good, that's one step ahead. Then maybe you don't want to help anybody, but you just refrain from harming anybody, that's another step. Then maybe you feel ready to help just a little bit, if it doesn't harm you at all, if there is nothing to lose.

Even if this is what you are doing, it doesn't mean that you are not a Bodhisattva, that you are not abiding by your Bodhisattva's vows. The main thing is your intention, your direction. What you are doing is taking a decision as to the direction in which you want to go. As to the pace, it is up to you. So, while you are saying the actual text of the vows, you try to generate a sense of commitment to going in that direction.

After we have taken the Bodhisattva's vows, we rejoice at the good thing we have done:

> *Now my life is fruitful - I have truly achieved a human existence. Today*
> *I have been born into the family of Buddhas. Today I have become a son*
> *of the Buddhas. Now, no matter what is required of me, I will act in*
> *conformity with my kindred family and will never do anything which might*
> *sully this faultless noble line.*

This time I have made my human life fruitful because I took this decision to develop Bodhicitta. I decided to become a Bodhisattva in order to become an enlightened being, so as to be able to help all sentient beings including myself. So now I have done something very good, something I hadn't done before. In the past, I have been trying to help myself, but because I didn't know how to do it, I didn't even succeed in helping myself, let alone helping others. Now, by taking the decision to help all others, I am also helping myself, I have decided to walk the path which will benefit myself and others, therefore I can congratulate myself for having done a very good thing.

By taking this decision to walk in the footprints of the Bodhisattvas, I have become a member of the Sangha, of the family of the Buddhas, somebody who is certain to become an enlightened being, a Buddha. Therefore I am like a "baby Buddha", or a prince who will soon succeed (his father) and become a king. Therefore, by taking that vow, that commitment to go in that direction, I've made a great decision, and I should behave in a way befitting that kind of profession. I should not stain my Bodhisattva family. As I consider myself as a Bodhisattva, I will become a "good" Bodhisattva, I will not make people feel or think that Bodhisattvas are not good. I will not be like a "blot" in this pure family.

The next thing is to rejoice for others:

> *Today, in the presence of all the protectors of beings I invite all beings to be my guests at the great celebration of Buddhahood and of happiness until then. Therefore gods, semi-gods and others, all truly rejoice!*

So today I have made a decision in front of all the great beings, and that decision is to invite all the sentient beings to the ultimate happiness. Therefore I have made a great commitment and I have started a great project, the biggest project ever. So all who know about it, other beings, spirits, Bodhisattvas of the past, all should rejoice! Then, at the end, you say a prayer that is a dedication. You dedicate all the virtues, the positive karma, the results of your taking this great commitment for the following purpose :

> *May the precious bodhicitta arise in those in whom it has not yet arisen.*
> *Wherever it has arisen, may it never deteriorate but grow more and more.*
> *Never cut off from bodhicitta, engaged in deeds conducive to enlightenment and perfectly cared for by all the Buddhas, may we give up harmful actions.*
> *May whatever Bodhisattvas have in mind to benefit beings come true.*
> *May whatever the protectors wish to happen to beings happen.*
> *May all beings be happy and may all states of suffering be emptied.*
> *May every prayer of the Bodhisattvas, wherever they are, come true.*

This is the dedication, and then, to conclude, you say what we call the Four Immeasurables or Four Limitless Contemplations[16]:

May all beings have happiness and the causes of happiness
May they all be free from suffering and the causes of suffering
May they never be deprived of true happiness devoid of any suffering
May they abide in great impartiality, free from attachment to loved ones and
aversion to others.

This ends the Bodhisattva's vows. You say this prayer with a genuine aspiration 3 times, or many times. Sometimes people recite this prayer 100,000 times.

Questions

Sometimes, we have a good intention, we want to benefit others, but either it is not perceived in a positive way, or the result is negative. Sometimes also we want to benefit one person. However that person is not alone but in relation with other persons, and benefiting one will harm somebody else. So what can we do?

Of course, we cannot control everything. So we do our best and hope for the best. We cannot see everything, but at least we can act with a good intention and a clean heart. Sometimes it benefits, sometimes it does not. Even if it does not bring benefit, we did it with a good intention and we can do no more than that.

If we do something for one, two, three or four people, one may benefit more than the others., One may not benefit at all, they might even be harmed, but that may not be your fault. Sometimes you give food to people, and they fall ill, but that may not be the fault of the person who gave the food.

The Four Foundations are contemplated at the beginning of every session of Ngöndro. We sit and we read the lines of the text, trying to remind ourselves, to be conscious, to rekindle our awareness of these truths and to feel inspired by them. Then from Refuge onwards, we usually count the number of times we do each practice.
In order to receive the Mahamudra teachings, we usually do these preliminaries 108,000 times each: - 100,000 Taking Refuge plus 108,000 prostrations; 108,000

Vajrasattva purifications; 108,000 Mandala offerings. Of course, it does not mean that after having done all this you become different. Maybe it does not change you, maybe you became even worse. You cannot make a rule about something that cannot be measured, but some sort of guideline has to be established and the tradition has been that if you do 100,000 of each of these preliminaries, you are ready to receive the Mahamudra teachings. You may not be ready after you have done all this, and it is not always true that people cannot receive the Mahamudra teachings without having done all this, but the tradition has been that the Mahamudra teachings were not given to those who had not completed 100,000 of each.

I have also found that people have difficulties doing these things because it needs a lot of patience, a lot of determination, and if they don't understand what they are doing, they feel they are wasting their time doing something completely useless. Usually, what we do is, we do a prostration at the same time as we say the Refuge prayer and we repeat both these actions 108,000 times. I can't say exactly whether it is the right or the most suitable preliminary for Westerners, but this has been the tradition so far, and the tradition has demonstrated certain value. This is the way it has been done for many generations, and by doing it this way, many great people have appeared, they have gained great benefits and realisations. Therefore, the tradition is validated by experience.

If some people want to practise the Ngöndro it might also be good to practise together as a group because they may help and support each other. It is also said that if a group of people do one good deed, each of them gets the whole benefit of doing that good action, the benefit is not divided among them. If all of you together save one person, each of you gets the positive karma, the positive results of saving a person. If all of you together do something wrong, each of you gets the whole negative result, it doesn't have less result. If for instance they have done together 100,000 Vajrasattva mantras, it is as if each one of them had done 100,000 Vajrasattva mantras. Therefore it is very good to practise together, unless there are obstacles to it of course.

Notes:

1.   Lineage of Mahamudra : Buddha Vajradhara > Tilopa (988 - 1069) > Naropa (1016 - 1100) > Marpa (1012 - 1097) > Milarepa (1040 - 1123) > Gampopa (1079 - 1153) > Dusum Khyenpa (1st Karmapa) > the succession of Karmapas.

2.   Vinaya : part of the Tripitaka (Indian Buddhist Canon), or "3 baskets". The Vinaya pitaka codifies the rules of behaviour and ethics.

3.   Dharma protectors (Dharmapala) (Chö kyong / chos skyong) : can be either powerful non-humans converted to Buddhism, who have vowed to protect the Buddhist doctrine and its practitioners, or wrathful manifestations of the Buddhas' activity.

4.   Realised Sangha : the Sangha of Bodhisattvas.

5.   Mandala (kyil khor / dkyil 'khor): center and surrounding, it can mean different things :-
     - a symbolic graphic representation of a tantric deity's realm of existence
     - or a mental visualisation or a graphic representation serving as a support for meditation
     - or a representation of the entire universe
     - or the offering of the universe

6.   Sakya Pandita (1182 - 1251 AD) Renowned Master of the Sakya School of Tibetan Buddhism.

7.   The 3 Jewels : Buddha, Dharma and Sangha.

8.   The 2 Rupakayas are the Nirmanakaya and the Sambhogakaya.

9.   10 bhumis : stages of realisation and activities through which a Bodhisattva progresses on their way to Buddhahood.

10. 5 paths : different stages of the path towards Enlightenment. The 3rd path, (vision or seeing) corresponds to   the 1st bhumi. For a more detailed explanation of paths and bhumis, see teaching on Gampopa's Dagpo Thargyen.

11. 11th bhumi : Buddhahood, Enlightenment.

12. 4 Activities :
     1) Pacifying (outer negativities as famine, illness, conflicts, and inner negativities like negative emotions)
     2) Increasing (outer positive situations and inner spiritual realization)
     3) Magnetising (mastery over outer and inner energies)
     4) Subjugating (all negative forces)

13. Channels : refers to the belief in the existence of a "subtle" body, of which constituents are channels, in which circulate "winds" of energy and "drops". These channels can be blocked , impeding the good circulation of energies.

14. Dewachen : Pure Land of Great Felicity of Buddha Amithaba.
     A Pure Land (shing kam/ zhing khams) is:
     - a place manifested through the wishes of a Buddha or a great Bodhisattva, where beings can be
       born and progress towards enlightenment without ever falling back in lower realms of existence.
     - or any place when it is perceived as a pure manifestation.

15. Chang chub : (byang chub sems)

16. The 4 "Immeasurables" are : love, compassion, joy, and equanimity.

2. Dorjé Sempa (Purification)

The Dorjé Sempa (Tibetan) or Vajrasattva (Sanskrit) practice is a very important practice which is used as the most effective purification or healing method in Vajrayana Buddhism. It is used by all Tibetan Buddhist schools. All of them do the same Vajrasattva practice, and it is supposed to be the most effective of all purification techniques. The technique behind it is more or less the same as that of all healing practices that we do through meditation.

Now why Dorjé Sempa? Why this deity? The Buddha said that Vajrasattva, or Dorjé Sempa, is the Buddha who, right from the time he first generated Bodhicitta until he became an enlightened being, dedicated all his activities, all his positive deeds as a Bodhisattva to the healing and purification of all beings. His main wish, his sole aspiration, was to be able to heal and purify all sentient beings. Therefore, his spontaneous power of healing and purification is the greatest.

If from the time you become a Bodhisattva you have a strong aspiration to grant, for instance, long life or success, or protection for all beings-and you say a prayer in that way and dedicate all your practices towards that aim-then we believe that you will become a Buddha with that particular power. This is why, even now, when we say prayers, it is so important to make very vast and grand prayers. It is important to make prayers in the most spacious and generous way. Dorjé Sempa made the specific prayer to be able to purify all the negative deeds, and thereby eliminate all their negative results, like illnesses and sufferings that come from those negative deeds. This is because, as you know, all the negative things that happen to us come out of our negative deeds.

It is believed that to practise Dorjé Sempa has a very special, an unequalled power to eliminate all our negative karma and the negative results of that karma. What we actually do is very simple. First, there is the visualisation of Dorjé Sempa:

On a lotus and moon seat above my head is my guru, Dorjé Sempa, white in colour and exquisitely adorned. Seated in the Vajra posture, he has one face, two arms, the right hand holding a Vajra, and the left one a bell.

This is the form you think of. A little above your head, about one foot, you visualise a big lotus flower, and on top of that lotus flower, there is a moon disc, and on top of it sits Vajrasattva. But he is not just the Vajrasattva deity, he is inseparable from your own root guru (if you have one) and he is also one with all the enlightened beings. The Vajrasattva you have visualised is not like a kind of sculpture, or painting, but he is fully alive, with all the qualities of a Buddha. He has a completely enlightened mind, unlimited compassion and wisdom, and he radiates love, compassion, joy, power and energy in the form of different coloured rays of light. Vajrasattva is white, and he is decorated with all the ornaments of a Sambhogakaya Buddha. When we talk of a Buddha in the Dharmakaya form, it means that he is represented as totally naked, without ornaments, without any clothes. When we talk of a Buddha in the Sambhogakaya form, he is represented as an Indian prince or princess, in the form of enjoyment, very beautiful, young, with 30 different ornaments, very rich, with gold, silver and diamonds. There are also wrathful forms of Sambhogakaya. And when we talk of a Nirmanakaya form, it is the form of Shakyamuni Buddha, with the monk's robes and a begging bowl.

So Vajrasattva is in the Sambhogakaya form, sitting cross-legged, with a Vajra in his right hand, and a drilbu - or bell - in his left hand.

You may not be able to visualise him completely clearly and as much as you wish, but it doesn't matter. The main thing is that you feel the energy. It is also good if you can visualise certain parts, sometimes the face, sometimes the energy, the lights, or the form, or the mantra with a white Hung[1] in Dorjé Sempa's heart. But most important is the feeling that Dorjé Sempa is the embodiment of energy, of compassionate wisdom, of all the positive things, because what we are actually trying to do through all these practices is to identify with these qualities. We try to get out of our constant tendency to feel bad, negative, frustrated and tense. Therefore, if you think of all these positive qualities, of these positive energies, even if you cannot identify with them, your mind concentrates on them, and therefore you develop more positive feelings. This is very important. The figure is just symbolic, but the main point is your concentration on these positive energies, to get absorbed in those positive qualities.

When our visualisation is established, we think that from the heart of the Dorjé Sempa above our head, rays of light emanate in all ten directions, going all over the universe, inviting the assembly of "jnana-sattvas" or "yeshé sempa"[2] - which means that the blessings, the energy, the power and mind of all the enlightened beings is invited to dissolve into Dorjé Sempa. In this way, we become more confident that this kind of energy, the union of all the positive energies, is actually present above our head. Actually, the most important thing is to maintain the concentration throughout the practice. When we do this, we are serving two purposes:

1. We practice the calming-down meditation through keeping our mind fully concentrated in one place,

2. We develop compassion and the positive side of ourselves by wholeheartedly absorbing our mind in positive aspects.

As I said before, the only way to become more positive, to develop the positive, is to think less and less of the negative while thinking more and more of the positive.

We now say a prayer to Dorjé Sempa :

> *My guru, Dorjé Sempa, I pray you, cleanse and purify the multitude of harmful deeds, obscurations, faults and transgressions leading to downfall, in myself and in all other beings, everywhere, to the end of space.*

We pray with genuine feeling that with Dorjé Sempa's help and our own strong aspiration, all our negative deeds and those of all the sentient beings may be purified. Following that supplication, we visualise the Hung on top of a moon disc in the heart centre of Dorjé Sempa. We should see Dorjé Sempa in a transparent, rainbow like form, not as a solid, opaque figure. Therefore we can see the Hung inside his body, surrounded by the Hundred Syllable Mantra, from which flows a stream of amrita. Amrita is a kind of nectar, of divine liquid, that contains the blessings, or the power, or the energy of Vajrasattva and his mantra, of our own purified nature. The mantra[3] around the Hung appears in very small, thin letters, as if they were written with one hair. When we recite the mantra, we visualise that drops of amrita stream from the mantra.

This stream of energy flows from the mantra, flows through Dorjé Sempa's body and enters our own body through the fontanel or "Brahma aperture". As it flows down through our body, we should feel that all our negative deeds, all our negative karma and its results, obscurations, illnesses, pain, blockages, everything is completely cleansed. From the head to the toes, all the negativities leave our body, and all its parts are cleansed from within. Even the causes of the negativities, the mind poisons, the negative emotions are completely purified. As we think of this process, of the nectar running like water in our body and purifying everything, we try to feel we are becoming more and more joyful and blissful. What enters into us is nectar, and nectar is supposed to be a substance that gives a sensation of warmth, pleasure and bliss when we touch it. When we are completely purified, our body is like an empty bottle that fills with nectar, we feel there is nothing negative in us any more, we experience an unearthly bliss, and we try to concentrate on that.

Sometimes, it seems that people who do the Dorjé Sempa practice tend to concentrate more on the negative than on the positive, they think of all the negative deeds they did, they feel and think more of the negative side, but that is not good, that is unnecessary. Try to feel the positive side because now the negative is finished, it is purified, eliminated. This is not just for ourselves, but for all sentient beings. Of course, first we need to concentrate on our own purification, but at the same time, we try to think and feel that this is not only happening to ourselves but to all sentient beings.

While thinking of this, we recite the mantra:

Om Bendza Sato Samaya Manupalaya Bendza Sato Tenopa Titra Drito
Mébawa Suto Kayo Mébawa Supo Kayo Mébawa Anurakto Mébawa
Sarwa Siddhi Mentra Yatsa Sarwa Karma Sutsamé Tsitam Shiri ya Guru
Hung Ha Ha Ha Ha Ho Bhagawan Sarwa Tatagata Bendza Mamé
Muntsa Bendza Bhawa Maha Samaya Sato Ah

This is not really the way the Sanskrit is read, but it is the way the Tibetans read Sanskrit!

After this Hundred Syllable Mantra, which you can recite as often as you wish, we recite the Six Syllable Mantra, which is a shorter form of the 100 Syllable Mantra:

Om Bendza Sato Hung

At the end, when we have recited the mantra and done the Dorjé Sempa practice as often as we want to, we conclude by joining our hands at the level of our heart and saying the following prayer:

Protector, unknowingly and out of stupidity, I have violated and broken
my commitments. My guru and protector, give me Refuge. Highest one,
Vajra-holder, whose nature is the greatest compassion, I take Refuge in
you, leader of beings. I confess and repent all breaches of the principal
and secondary commitments related to body, speech and mind. Please grant
your blessing that the multitude of harmful deeds, obscurations, faults and
transgressions leading to downfall may be cleansed and purified.

Dorjé Sempa is one and the same with all the Buddhas, all the protectors. "Protector" here doesn't mean the "Dharma protectors", it is one of the names of the Buddha. The Tibetan word "gönpo" could be translated as "Lord". It applies to somebody who has the power and willingness to protect.

Due to our confusion and ignorance, we have done many bad things. We now realise how badly we behaved and that these negative actions will have negative results. This is not what we want; we want positive results. Therefore we regret what we did under the power of our delusion, we take the firm resolution not to do it again and we ask to be purified of all those negativities. Even the good things we tried to do by taking vows, samayas[4] and commitments,- we were unable to keep them due to our ignorance, our inability, and other different other reasons like aversion and attachment, so we broke our engagements. We now express our strong wish to completely get rid of these mind poisons, of the negative things we did and the positive we did not. Therefore we take Refuge in Vajrasattva and we supplicate him to help us. The text then says:

> *Dorjé Sempa gives me release, melts into light and dissolves into me,*
> *making us "not two".*

When we say this, we feel that we are completely purified, that whatever negativities we have are purified, and what was not completely fulfilled is now fulfilled.

Now we think that we become exactly like Vajrasattva. The Vajrasattva we have visualised melts into light, dissolves into us. Our Vajrasattva nature, our pure Buddha nature has been awakened because, as said already, the temporary defilements are the only obstructions keeping us from becoming fully enlightened. So now, since we have completely purified our negativities, we fully become Vajrasattva himself. We try to look at ourselves as being Vajrasattva, to feel ourselves in that state of complete purity, and this is the end of the Vajrasattva practice.

It is a very good healing method and it has some effects, if we do it long enough. It is not difficult to do, but whether it will have an actual effect or not depends on whether we actually do it or not.

Questions

Rinpoche, regarding visualisation, I always have a problem: Do I see it in front of me or do I feel myself like that? When you say for instance that we should visualise ourselves as Vajrasattva, do I see myself as Vajrasattva in front of me, or do I feel myself as Vajrasattva?

First you visualize Vajrasattva in front of you facing you in the sky above you or on top of your head facing the same way you do, which ever you feel easier. Then later you visualise yourself as Vajrasattva, so if you want to look at yourself from any angle, it is up to you ! Your actual body becomes Vajrasattva. You are not seeing it with your eyes, because you cannot see yourself completely.

Can I dedicate the merits of this practice for one person in particular?

Usually, the Buddhist way of dedication is that, even if we want to dedicate it to one person, we don't just do that, we dedicate it to all beings, because when we do so, the merit becomes even more, it multiplies. Then we make a second dedication to the person for whom we actually want to do it.

Notes:

1. A picture of Dorjé Sempa is useful.
2. Yeshe Sempa : beings who embody perfect non-dual wisdom.
3. Mantra : syllables charged with energy, manifestation of different aspects of Buddhahood. Mantras protect the mind from distraction and dispersion and serve as support for meditation.
4. Samaya : sacred pledge or vows, commitments linked to a Vajrayana practice.

3. The Mandala Offering

We now come to the third of the Special Practices which is the Mandala Offering. In the actual practice of Buddhism, there are only two things to do :

1. To purify, get rid of and eliminate all our negativities, and
2. To develop and increase all our positive sides.

If we want to summarise the whole of Buddhism into one sentence, it is just this, trying to get rid of all the negative and develop the positive. This is what we do with these practices. With the Vajrasattva practice, we get rid of all the negativities, and with the mandala offering, we try to accomplish, to accumulate all the positive things. It is as simple as that.

Mahayana Buddhism teaches the "Six Paramitas" as the method to develop our more positive side. If you really develop the Six Paramitas, or Six Transcendental Wisdoms, they include all the positive things we need to develop. As you all know, these Six Paramitas are:

1. Generosity,
2. Good conduct,
3. Patience,
4. Diligence
5. Meditation,
6. Wisdom,

Out of these Six Paramitas, we start with generosity, which is maybe the easiest of all six. It is the most important, the first thing to do, and it serves as a basis for all the other Paramitas. Therefore we first try to develop generosity, which doesn't mean that we only develop generosity since all Paramitas are actually interrelated. If we develop one, we also develop all the others. If we look at it more closely, we find all Six Paramitas in any one of them.

However, when we say that we start with generosity, it means that the emphasis is on generosity. Generosity is the opposite of attachment. The main problem, the essence, the root cause of all our samsaric sufferings, of our samsaric state of mind is aversion and attachment. Therefore, our main, real practice, is to try to deal with aversion and attachment. In the Ngöndro, we deal with aversion through the Vajrasattva practice, whereas we deal with attachment through the Mandala Offering. With these two, we are actually covering the essential practice, because there is in fact nothing more to do. If we get rid of aversion and attachment, or if we know how to deal with both, we actually clear our confusion, as these two are the basis of ignorance. When that is cleared, then ... we have "done it"!

Although we say that these are the "preliminaries", they are not just something we have to do at the beginning and then forget about it. They are actually all we need to do! In all the other practices, even when we come to the actual Mahamudra, there is nothing else to do but to deal with aversion and attachment. Therefore this is very simple, maybe sometimes so simple that we find it a little strange, but if we really look at it, if we can really integrate it into our experience, not just as a ritual, but as a real experience. Then it is very deep and meaningful.

Through offering what we are attached to, what we think is ours, what we cling to and cannot free ourselves from, we train our mind in letting go, in giving up. What we offer is not something we don't want and therefore give away, but something we treasure very much, and it is with great respect and great openness that we offer it. This is why we call it a "mandala offering", or the offering of the universe. This is not something you can't do, we can all learn to do this.

There is the story of Anathapindika that may demonstrate this. "Anatha" means "without protection", and "Pindika" means "provider of food". That name was given to him afterwards. But before he became famous for his generosity, he was very stingy, very miserly, although he was very rich. He used to attend the Buddha's teachings, he listened to them every day. Buddha sometimes talked about generosity, about giving, and the positive karma of giving. One day, Anathapindika came to see the Buddha to tell him that he usually found the teachings very nice, but that giving was something he just couldn't do.

> "If I give even a little bit, I feel a great pain! I can't manage it,
> it's impossible!"
> "Well, if you really try, you can do it." said the Buddha.
> "No, it can't be done!"
> "Can you give something to yourself?" asked Buddha
> "Oh yes! That's not a problem."
> "Then all right", said Buddha, "go back home, take something
> rather valuable in one hand, give it to the other hand and say
> 'take it', and do the same again and again."

So Anathapindika went home, maybe a little amused with the idea. He took a golden coin in his right hand and gave it to his left hand, saying "Take it". Then he gave it back to the right hand saying "Take it ". He did this exercise again and again, and slowly he opened up, and didn't mind giving away little things any more. He invited Buddha and his monks for a meal. He became more and more generous, and after some time, he was giving food to the hungry, building hospitals for both people and animals, and places where travellers could stay and eat. He become known as Anathapindika, the most generous person one could think of. This is how we can train ourselves.

When we do the mandala offering, training our mind is the most important thing. If we push ourselves too much (in our everyday life, if for instance we try to give too much) before we are mentally prepared for it, we may regret it afterwards, and even end up with the opposite attitude. Therefore it is very important, even essential, to first train our minds in this way. This is what we do through the 37 point Mandala Offering.

When you read the text, you may find it strange, but what we are actually trying to do is to imagine all the most precious, the most wonderful, the most miraculous things and then offering them. On top of what is described, you may add whatever you think of as very nice, what you are very much attached to, what you want for yourself. You can include all that, and then you offer it. This is not restricted to the practice of the Mandala Offering, but in your everyday life also, you can practise this as a kind of exercise. When you are very much attracted to something, when you want it for yourself and you can't get it, you make a mental offering of it, and in this way, you get less frustrated, you can let it go.

First of all, when you offer a mandala, you visualise the Refuge Tree (as we discussed before) in front of you, as is described here:

> My guru is in front of me, in the centre of the sky. Before him are the yidams, to his right the Buddhas, behind him the dharma and to his left the realised Sangha. All of them are accompanied by many others like them. In between their seats are oceans of dharma protectors. I am in the presence of all the Precious Ones - the perfect and excellent "field of accumulation".

Then you imagine that you are offering all the most precious things to all the enlightened and great beings. When you actually perform the practice, you take a "mandala plate" in the left hand, take rice (or anything) in your right hand and wipe the plate, three times clockwise and one time counter-clockwise, while reciting the Vajrasattva 100 syllable mantra. While doing this, you think that this action cleanses your mind of all negative thoughts, negative emotions and negative karma. Then you say:

Om Bendza Bhumi Ah Hung

You sprinkle grain on the plate, thinking it is the golden earth ('bhumi' means the earth). Then you say:

Om Bendza Rekhe Ah Hung

You drop rice around the edge of the plate, and afterwards you put piles of grain around it, (while reading the text and imagining the different offerings). In the short mandala offering, there are just 5 piles of grain, whilst in the long version, there are 37 points. The elements enumerated in the text come from the Indian tradition, they are what were supposed to be the most wonderful, the most miraculous things in the universe, and on top of them, you can offer all that you yourself consider most wonderful.

> In the centre of a ring of iron mountains is the king of mountains, Mount Meru[1]. In the east is Lupakpo, to the south Dzambuling, to the west Balangchö and to the north Draminyen[2]. Lu and Lupak, Ngayap and Ngayap Chen, Yoden and Lamchodro, Draminyen and Draminyen Jida[3]. A jewel mountain, a wish-granting tree, a cow giving milk as much as one wants, crops that need no cultivation. The precious wheel, the precious jewel, the precious queen, the precious minister, the precious elephant, the precious horse, the precious general, a vase containing inexhaustible treasures. Goddesses of beauty, goddesses offering garlands, songs, dances, flowers, incense, lights and perfumes. The sun, the moon, a canopy of jewels, banners of victory flying over all directions. Amidst all these things are displayed the finest and most enjoyable possessions of gods and men, nothing being omitted, in far greater number than the dust particles of innumerable universes.

> These I offer to all the gurus, yidams, Buddhas, bodhisattvas and the multitude of Dakas, dakinis, male and female dharma protectors. Out of your great compassion, please accept these offerings for the sake of all beings, and having accepted them, pray grant your blessing.

Then we say the short mandala offering:

> The ground is sprinkled with scented water, strewn with flowers and adorned with Mount Meru, the four continents, the sun and the moon. I imagine this to be a Buddha-field. Through making such an offering, may all beings abide in the Pure Lands.

This is the main mandala offering that we repeat 100,000 times.
The text continues:

> *I imagine that I offer a million, a hundred thousand million, a hundred*
> *billion mandalas all gathered into this one mandala, to all the Buddhas and*
> *Bodhisattvas in the ten directions and the three times, to all the Gurus and*
> *Vajra Teachers, to all the Yidams and their entourages and to the Sugatas*[4] *of*
> *the three times.*
>
> *I pray that out of your great compassion, you may consider me with kindness*
> *and accept this offering of mine. Having accepted it, please grant your blessing*
> *that I may be able to lead all the sentient beings to a completely pure land.*

After having thus prayed, we say the mantra:

> *Om Mendala Pudza Megha Samudra Saparana Samayé Ah Hung*

This mantra multiplies a million times the offering that we have already made, and we now think that the offering has been accomplished.

This is the main practice we do again and again, until our mind becomes pure, more open, until all our stinginess, all our attachments become non-existent. Then we pray and dedicate the merits of our practice:

> *Now that I have offered this good and pleasing mandala, may there be no*
> *obstacles on the path to enlightenment, may I achieve the realisation of the*
> *Sugatas of the three times, neither falling into the illusion of existence, nor*
> *that of non-existence, and may I liberate all beings in numbers as vast as*
> *infinite space.*
>
> *To all the Gurus who have perfectly achieved the three kayas, I present the*
> *outer, inner and secret offerings and the offering of suchness. As you accept*
> *my body, possessions and all animate and inanimate manifestations, I pray*

you to grant me the unsurpassable supreme spiritual accomplishment. Please
bestow upon me the supreme accomplishment of Mahamudra.
I prostrate, offer and purify, I rejoice, request and pray. Whatever small
virtues I thus gather, I dedicate to perfect great enlightenment. Through this
offering of all my possessions, as well as those of all beings innumerable as
space is infinite, may all beings perfectly complete the two accumulations.

The field of accumulation melts into light, fuses into me, and we are of one taste.

This means that at the end, we feel the Refuge Tree in front of us melts into light and dissolves into us, becomes one with us, and that is the end of the Mandala Practice.

———◆———

Notes:

1. Mount Meru : mythological giant mountain, centre and axis of the whole universe according to the Hindu cosmology.
2. The 4 continents
3. The eight subcontinents on each side of each continent
4. Sugatas : "Blissfully Gone", a title given to the Buddhas

4. Guru Yoga

INTRODUCTION

Guru Yoga is actually quite a simple practice, and to do it in a proper way requires a certain basic understanding.

The wrong attitude one encounters most frequently is that of people placing themselves under the domination of the guru, viewing their guru as their master and themselves as his or her slave. They do whatever the guru tells them to and, as they generally expect gurus to be quite unpredictable and strange, they are not surprised to be asked to do lots of funny things, through which they are convinced they will progress and ultimately become like their guru. This is not a healthy attitude, but perhaps understandable!

Of course, usually, when we talk about the guru/disciple relationship, we look at it from the ideal point of view. If an ideal disciple meets an ideal guru, they would have an ideal relationship, but people tend to mistake this ideal situation for what should actually be, and think it should be like that all the time. However, they discover after a while that the guru is not an ideal guru, that the disciple is not an ideal disciple, and that their relationship is far from ideal too.

This evokes for me the Western concept of falling in love. In the West you have this very romantic idea of falling in love. When you fall in love, the stars shine brighter, flowers blossom wherever you step, roses fall from the sky, rainbows appear above your head and you enter a completely different realm where you will be happy together ever after.

This is not the right attitude because it just does not work. Guru Yoga should be viewed as different from the actual guru/student relationship. We practice Guru Yoga as an ideal because it is a practice, an exercise. The guru/student relationship is something else. I don't mean that you should not have faith in your guru. It is good to have faith in our guru, but with an open mind and open eyes. We cannot completely, blindly trust any person from whom we receive teachings. It is unnecessary and it is not good for the guru or for the student. Therefore, in the actual guru/student relationship, it is very important to gradually develop confidence and trust.

I think you will not be able to find a completely perfect guru, because to find one, you would firstly have to be a completely perfect student yourself. If our way of seeing things is imperfect, how can we find somebody perfect? A perfect guru may exist, I am not denying the possibility of that, but they are very difficult to find.

This does not mean that you should not have a guru, because we are talking here about a question of balance. If the benefit is greater than the negative aspect, it is acceptable. I think it is advisable to have a good guru, maybe not perfect, but somebody a bit better than us, whom we can trust and open to, from whom we can get inspiration and a better understanding. The main thing is to find out whether he or she is a genuine practitioner of Dharma. If it is the case, you cannot completely go wrong, nor be completely misled.

In order to find out, we need to know what the genuine practice of Dharma is. If we know a little what Dharma is, then we will know whether someone is genuinely practising Dharma or not. Of course, ideally, the higher and purer perception we have of our guru, the better it is and the quicker we will progress. It is said, and it is true, that if we see our guru as a Buddha, as a completely enlightened being, we will become one ourselves. If we see our guru as a very learned and highly qualified person, that is the result we will achieve. But if we see our guru as very ordinary, just like us, we will remain as we are.

I think it is the same thing with teachers or parents. If you think your teacher cannot teach you anything, you will not learn anything from him. How can you learn from a person you do not respect? The more we respect the teacher, the more we respect the teachings, and vice versa. The way we see our teacher and the teachings has a profound effect on the way we receive the teachings and the instructions.

To find a guru that we consider as highly qualified is very important because it will speed up our progress on the path. This is the core of the student/guru relationship. If we believe our guru is somebody we can trust, from whom we can learn something, then our own state of mind, our own reaction to the whole world changes.

The same thing happens in the parent/child relationship. Those children who have parents whom they can trust, with whom they have a good relationship, those who have received unconditional love, become very healthy in their mind. Those who have not had that kind of relationship usually encounter many more problems. In the same way, if we can find somebody whom we can trust, to whom we can open up, it is a very important step in itself, because we learn how not to be completely shut off from the world, how not to feel completely lonely. If we close ourselves up, we cannot confide, we cannot improve and we cannot change. This is why it is so important.

Questions

Didn't you say once that we can have many teachers but only one guru?

No, you can have many gurus, as far as I am concerned. I have more than one guru. Not only more than one guru, but more than one root guru. I consider that I have two root gurus, one is the XVI Karmapa, and the second is Dilgo Khyentsé Rinpoché. Also, I have countless gurus, I do not know how many, I never counted them, and I am not the only one. Most Tibetan Lamas have many gurus and it is not a problem.

Is it perhaps not a problem for the Lamas because the feel they are slaves of everybody, because of their Bodhisattva vow? When one takes the Bodhisattva vow, one already becomes the servant of all beings, does one have to become the slave of one's gurus on top of that? This seems very heavy to me.

I don't think I have to be the slave of anybody. I was using that word previously because one should **not** be like that! The Bodhisattva's attitude is to think that everybody is like himself, wishing happiness and disliking suffering. A Bodhisattva thinks he has to help everybody to get the best. He genuinely tries to learn how to get out of sufferings himself, in order to help all others do the same. A Bodhisattva trains in order to help and he or she will help as much as he or she can. By helping others, we help ourselves. It is not a question of neglecting one's own welfare. If you are a great Bodhisattva and have no problems yourself, then you will of course devote all your attention to others.

Now as to the guru, the main thing I am trying to explain is that how much you are devoted to the guru depends on your own perception. If you are absolutely sure that the guru is a completely enlightened being, that whatever he/she says is right, whatever he/she asks you to do is good for yourself and good for everybody, if you have no doubt about that, then of course you will do it. It is natural. But otherwise, you may not do it. If you do not do something the guru tells you, you do not break any vow. The Dalai Lama usually says that if our guru tells us to do something, and we think it is not the right thing for us, we may tell him. I think that is right. There is no breach of Samaya. I am not giving my own opinion, I am actually quoting from the texts.

How should we ask a teacher to become our guru?

Just like that! "Hello, would you become my guru?"

Is there some respectful way of doing it?

Well, there is no procedure that is recorded in the books or anywhere, but I think you would naturally do it respectfully. The way you express that respect does not matter that much. It depends on your culture. In the East, people bow down and show many marks of respect, but it is not necessarily more respectful than a handshake. It is more a question of inner attitude than the way of expressing it. The Indian and Tibetan way is to show outward respect, we prostrate, sit on our knees, make ourselves very small, but while doing this, we may at the same time harbour nasty thoughts. One of the ways of showing respect to the teacher is to have him sit on a throne. Sometimes, people in the West are disturbed by this, but it is out respect for the teachings.

In the East, there are many gurus. It is easy to meet them and make your choice. Our quest is more difficult in the West. Do we have to search for our guru, or should we accept one of the lamas that we have the opportunity to meet?

Yes, to search is what we usually do. We search for one, but we do not keep on searching all the time. I have met people who told me: "I have been searching for a guru for 15 years and still I cannot find one. Please tell me when I will find this guru I am searching for." They are really impatient and tense. That is not necessary, you can take what comes, more or less, but it does not mean you do not have to keep on searching.

When you have found your guru, he is not always present. Is it true that there is a link that is established between the guru and the student, or is it just a romantic idea we get?

I think that it is not necessary to be always sitting with our guru, but to have a good communication with him is important. The guru is the person from whom we learn, so it is necessary to ask questions and to talk about our experience. It is not enough to say: "He is my guru," and that's all, We have to learn but not necessarily to be together all the time. Then there is something that is called the inner guru, about which I will talk later. That is most important. What we are talking about now is the outer guru.

Sometimes, people are too dependent on their guru. Not only in the West, sometimes also in the East. They ask his advice on everything, like what kind of colour they should paint their bathroom, and so on. This is not necessary. The guru's job is to try to teach his student how to actually stand on his/her own feet, to be independent as much as possible, to try to understand the Dharma and know how to practise by themselves. When you know how to practise, then you become more independent. That is the main teaching. It used to be like that in Tibet also. The guru would give teachings, and when the training was finished, he would send his students away to practise, sometimes to some very faraway places.

Of course there is a relationship. It is a heart relationship and therefore there is a certain element of emotion in it. I do not agree at all with a kind of professional relationship, I mean completely without emotions. Since it is a human relationship, emotions will always be involved. You have to like your guru, otherwise you wouldn't choose him as your guru, and so if you love your guru, I think it is all right. What really matters is that the guru should teach his students how to stand on their own feet.

Generally speaking, the guru is a teacher who has not only intellectual but some experiential understanding, some knowledge and realisation of the Dharma. It is not enough that he just knows the subject, he should actually practise the teachings, be genuinely training him/herself and live by the teachings. On top of this, he should have a genuine willingness to pass on to others the teachings that he/she has found helpful. He should also have some capacity to teach. These are the main qualifications of a guru or teacher. The concept that the guru is an absolute necessity is not found in all Buddhist traditions. In the Theravada, and even in the Mahayana traditions, although the teacher is very important, a greater emphasis is placed on the Dharma itself. In the Vajrayana, however, a greater importance is given to the teacher because its approach is more experiential.

The understanding of the texts and the words of the Buddha are very important, but they have to go hand in hand with the experience. It is impossible to get some experiential teachings from somebody who has had no experience, hence the importance of an experienced guru. The Vajrayana is not just about learning and teaching, there is something else, which could be called a heart to heart transmission. It is difficult to explain but I can illustrate it with the story of Tilopa and Naropa.

Naropa was a very great scholar, one of the greatest of the five most important professors of the Nalanda University. At that time, it was the custom or the tradition, that anybody could challenge the doctrine in an open debate, with the king of the country appointed witness and judge. Whoever lost the debate would become the follower of the winner. Therefore, at that time, to become a professor was much more difficult than now. Naropa was appointed "Gate Keeper of the North". He would debate with any challenger coming from the Northern direction of the University. He became very famous as one of the best scholars and he had many disciples.

One day, he was sitting in the sun on his veranda, reading a book, a very high tantric text. He was feeling very good about himself because he understood everything. Suddenly, a strange shadow fell on his book. He looked up and saw an old ugly lady standing beside him. She said: "You do not understand anything of this!" Naropa was shocked and surprised, but realised at once that it was actually true he understood the words, but not the experience. He asked her: "Who does understand?" The old lady answered: "My brother, Tilopa!" Leaving everything there, without even rolling up the text he was reading, Naropa left in search of Tilopa.

Eventually he found Tilopa and asked him to take him as a disciple, but Tilopa just stood up and walked away without even looking at him. Naropa followed him. This situation lasted for many years, during which Tilopa asked Naropa to do many completely crazy things. Finally, after undergoing many trials and hardships, coming close to death about 13 times, Naropa received the transmission. It happened without a single word being uttered.

One day, as Naropa was walking towards him, Tilopa became very angry, took his sandal off and threw it at him. Naropa was hit on the head and fainted. When he came to, he knew everything that Tilopa knew, he had the complete experience. He had known everything before intellectually, but now he had the actual experience.

This may not be a very good example because it is too extreme. It does not mean that it should happen like that for all of us, but this story illustrates the fact that there is something else, not just the teachings, the texts and the understanding of their meaning; there is also the experience. The guru is a medium to receive that experience.

From the Vajrayana point of view, we always talk about an outer and an inner guru. The outer guru is our teacher, and it is through the outer guru that we realise the inner guru. The inner guru is the actual, what we call the ultimate guru, the inner guru of Dharmakaya, which means our true nature.

Guru Yoga is a training to awaken the inner guru. Through our devotion to the outer guru, through his teachings and the practice of Guru Yoga, we come to realise the inner guru. This is a practice of devotion, of merging and of being, through which we learn how to be without concepts. We learn how to open up completely and how to surrender our ego. Through it, we can broaden ourselves, make ourselves non dual, so that we can experientially see, meet our inner guru or our inner light. That is why, from the Vajrayana point of view, to find the right guru is very important, but only as a medium to realise one's inner guru. The practice of Guru Yoga is therefore even more important.

From the Buddhist point of view, devotion is a strong inspiration, a very strong feeling of trust and benevolence. I think people do not understand this emotion very easily in the West. If you know somebody who is really helpful and always wants to do everything to benefit you, and nothing else, then what kind of feeling would you have for that person? That is the closest feeling to devotion. It is really difficult to "create" or "manufacture" devotion. It has to come of its own. It is a trust, a deep trust, knowing that only good things will come out of the relationship. Devotion arises from such a background or understanding. Those of us who have been in the presence of really great masters know that devotion is not something that you need to generate or to work on, it just comes. If you have not met such people then devotion is not so easy to understand.

In Tibet and India, there was a lot of devotion and respect towards the teachers, and progressively, in the modern world, that respect is being lost. I don't only blame the students for this; I think a great responsibility also lies with the teachers themselves. I have studied in a semi-modern system, as well as under the completely old system, which remained the same as in the eighth century. I can see the difference very strongly, and it is still in the process of changing. I think the teachers of our time, and I'm including myself here, do not have that real compassion that was so striking in teachers of the old tradition. My teachers from the old tradition had such a willingness to teach that we could go and meet them at 4 o'clock in the morning, or 10 in the evening, it did not matter.

Dilgo Khyentse Rinpoché, when he was over 80, used to start his day at 4 o'clock in the morning, he would give teachings, make pujas and many other things until lunch time. In the afternoon, he would teach a group of students, then work and teach till 10 o'clock at night. He would then go to bed, but we would still rush in to see him. He would come down the stairs, and without stopping to breathe, he would start teaching again. We never made an appointment and, never asked if he was too tired, we never even thought he might be tired at all. He was not the only teacher like this, there were so many like him. When you come into contact with such people, there is no need to analyse or examine, it is so apparent that they have no other motive except concern for your understanding. They are so completely without any selfishness that the devotion is not something you have to worry about, it is just there. For those who have had the opportunity to have a little connection with such beings, the practice of Guru Yoga becomes very strong, because the devotion is a powerful medium to develop insight into the inner guru or true nature.

Devotion is an emotion which is not an analytical process. It is not thoughts, it is not thinking, it is not concepts, it is just feeling, emotion. However, at the same time, it is not a negative emotion, like anger or attachment. It is completely positive and very vibrant, very clear and strong. It is not dull at all. Therefore, within that state of mind, of being, we can just look at our mind and it is more likely that we will experientially see the true nature of our mind, which is unaltered, beyond concepts. We remember our own guru and through the affection, the love and strong devotion we feel for him, we look back at our mind. This is how we might be able to see our true nature. Then there are different stages, we merge with our guru, we emerge as our true nature, and we try to "be" in that state, which is the enlightened state.

The empowerments are a very important part of Guru Yoga. They are the strongest and most important practice in Vajrayana and they are connected to Guru Yoga. Many people have received what are termed the seed empowerments, meaning that they are given a teaching and receive the blessings and permission to practise a particular teaching. It is only an introduction to a particular teaching that has to be taken as a path through regular practice. It is then called the path empowerment. In Guru Yoga, we actualise this empowerment because we receive it every time we practise it. This is why I emphasise the importance of Guru Yoga as training.

The actual practice of Guru Yoga is not difficult to understand.

How does the relationship of Teacher/student evolve when the Guru passes away?

When the guru dies, the relationship remains the same. From the Buddhist point of view, when the guru dies, it is believed that the guru's power becomes even stronger, and if he has very good students, they then become like him. There are lots of stories illustrating how students, one, two or many, are transformed after their guru's death. The guru's blessings do not disappear with him. You can still do the practice, and try to realise the inner guru, it remains the same. Of course, if you want to learn more, if you wish to ask questions, you can also take another guru, which does not mean you forsake your previous guru. That is possible, that can be done. In the Tibetan way of thinking; there is no "former" guru or teacher. We never feel that someone is our "former" teacher. If somebody has taught me something, he is my teacher, whose teaching has made me what I am now. Once somebody is our guru, he remains our guru.

When a guru passes away, his presence and our devotion do not vanish. In fact, usually, practically, it is advisable to do the Guru Yoga of a master of the past, like for instance, in this practice, Dorje Chang. It could be Gampopa, Milarepa, or the Karmapas, like Karma Pakshi. It is very seldom that we do the Guru Yoga of a living teacher. This is because we can easily see faults in a guru living in worldly situations, whereas we cannot see any faults in a guru who has passed away. Nothing can damage his image. Everything is already known about him, there will not be anything new coming up! Therefore, our devotion becomes stronger, more stable.

When we do the Guru Yoga of a guru who is no longer alive, we also include our living guru. Our visualisation takes the form of a guru who has passed away, or some deity, but our own present guru is also part of it. The visualisation is the embodiment of all our gurus, of the entire lineage, of all enlightened beings. It is not just one individual, but the embodiment, the unity of them all.

What is the link, the relationship between the disciples of the same guru?

They are called the "Vajra brothers and sisters". They are supposed to be very close, to have very harmonious relations and never fight with each other. If they do fight, it is a very bad thing, breaking a very important link. Usually, the disciples of a guru are supposed to help each other. They will discuss their practice together and the more advanced students will help the others.

What are the relationship of a disciple and the new reincarnation of his former teacher?

We could feel the same kind of devotion towards the new reincarnation although he may not be able to teach for a while.

THE PRACTICE TEXT

I have so far introduced the practice of Guru Yoga, now we will go directly to the text. This text, as you know, is the Mahamudra Guru Yoga, but whatever Guru Yoga we do, the general idea remains the same. Sometimes, this practice is not taken as a preliminary but as a main practice. The main practice of Mahamudra or Dzogchen is done along with Guru Yoga.

Even if our practice focuses on Guru Yoga, we start each session with the beginning of the Ngöndro: We think for a short while about the Four Foundations, take Refuge, develop Bodhicitta, do a few Vajrasattva purifications, offer a few mandalas, and then only concentrate on Guru Yoga.

In this text, it starts immediately with the visualisation of the guru. Two things always precede whatever visualisation we do: one is emptiness and the second is compassion. This is very much related to the understanding of the view and the actual Mahamudra teachings. As we do not have a perfect understanding of this yet, when we say here that everything dissolves into emptiness at this moment, we do it at an intellectual level only, we "think" of emptiness.

The commentary reads:

> *Meditate that everything is purified into emptiness by means of the*
> *Swabhava mantra.*

The mantra:

> *Om Svabhava Shuddha Sarva Dharma Svabhava Shuddho Ham,*

is the mantra of purification, of dissolution. When we talk about "emptiness", the true nature of everything, it does not mean that things are empty in the sense that they become nothing. We are talking here about an experience, not about a concept. It is a state of being which is completely clear and aware, without any confusion, clinging, or sense of duality. There is no need of duality, it is completely free. That experience is what we call the understanding of emptiness. Therefore, when we talk of emptiness here, it is an exercise to transform ourselves, to make us aware that our usual way of seeing, understanding and experiencing things is not the only one possible. The world and ourselves are not as solid and real as we think, it can be something else too if we want. Therefore we begin our practice with this mantra, and our usual way of seeing things dissolves, nothing remains.

Out of this "emptiness", we appear as Vajrayogini or Vajravarahi. Although it is not mentioned in this text, we can do Guru Yoga by visualising ourselves as Vajrayogini. What does Vajrayogini look like? She is a young and very beautiful red lady. You can visualise yourself like her even if you are a tall macho muscled man with beard and all! In the Vajrayana practices, we often visualise ourselves as different deities, sometimes male, sometimes female, sometimes very beautiful, and sometimes quite ugly. They can be tall or very short, black, blue, red or any colour, with two arms or many, I think it is a way of training our mind, of not being completely attached and clinging to our sense of reality, of identity as being this or that.

Here we view ourselves as Vajravarahi, or Dorjé Phagmo in Tibetan -"phagmo" actually means "pig" - a red lady, very beautiful, but having a pig's head on one side of her own head, and standing on a corpse. A corpse is usually considered as something not so nice, but here we are standing on a human corpse lying on a sun disk and a red lotus, holding a curved knife and a skull cup from which we are about to drink. This is also an exercise in diminishing our strong propensity to label things as good or bad, clean or dirty. In this visualisation, bad things are not bad, good things are not good. We try to cut off from those concepts of dirty, bad, negative, not wanted, good, very nice, wanted, and so forth.

Guru Yoga can also be done without visualising ourselves as anything in particular, we can just remain as we are and that is good enough. However, when we visualise ourselves as Vajravarahii, it is assumed that we have a yidam practice. In Vajrayana, there are many different tantras, and we usually have one particular tantra as our main practice. The yidam practice is our main practice or Sadhana of a deity.

In a Sadhana, all that is needed in the practice of Dharma has been concentrated. If we understand it properly, we will be aware that all these different elements are gathered in a compact way, like on a CD ROM disc. Most people in Tibet practice Vajrayana through a yidam practice. It is assumed here that we have a yidam and that this yidam is Vajravarahi because Milarepa, Marpa and many great Kagyu masters all had Vajravarahi as their yidam. Therefore, in the Kagyu School, it is the tradition to visualise ourselves as Vajravarahi, because it is believed that we receive in this way the blessings of the lineage.

It is also sometimes explained that if, in the beginning, we just see ourselves as usual, we keep our strong attachment to our deluded way of seeing everything, whereas if we visualise ourselves as a yidam, a purer level of being, it may be easier to develop a new way of seeing, which might help us get the understanding. When we visualise ourselves as a deity, we do not only try to look different, we also try to feel as an enlightened being, and whatever his or her form may be. This is the most important thing. We are trying to feel, with our limited understanding, like an enlightened being. We may not know completely what it feels like, but we can imagine it to some extent.

We have an idea that an enlightened being has complete wisdom, feels complete compassion, unlimited joy and is completely free of sufferings. At least we have a certain understanding, an idea, an image of enlightenment, so we try to feel like that. In a way, what we are is what we feel like, therefore if we feel more and more like an enlightened being, then, maybe, slowly, we may become one. If I feel I am useless, the worst and ugliest person in the world, and nobody loves me, then I become like that. I start hating myself, and I react to others with the certainty that they dislike me too and are even ready to harm me. My reactions towards people change, the way I walk, sit and behave all reflect my inner attitude. On the other hand, if you think that you are someone, rather nice and beautiful, that people like you, that you are capable, then you feel good, you are more confident and you actually become like that. Not only do you change yourself, but other people react differently to you. You react in a more direct, honest way and people will naturally feel attracted to you. Such changes can even happen from moment to moment, within the same person. Sometimes we feel very happy and self-confident whereas a few hours later, we may feel sad and depressed. We can often see somebody's mood from afar.

Here we try to feel not only like a "smart fellow", but even like an "enlightened fellow", with lots of joy, happiness, understanding and compassion. That visualisation of ourselves is the first step.

It is also said that we have selected this particular female yidam Vajravarahi because the female energy, the female part of our energy is more open, and has the sharpest receptivity.

Having arisen as Vajravarahi, we now visualise the guru or the Refuge Tree on top of our head, or in front of us. The text describes it as follows:

> *On a lotus, sun and moon above my head is my root guru, Dorjé Chang, exquisitely adorned. He sits in the Vajra posture, holding a vajra and bell in his crossed hands. Gurus and precious ones are gathered around him in great numbers, some above each others, some in great clusters.*

If we are sitting, it is easier to visualise this in front of us, whereas if we are walking, it is better to imagine it above our head, facing in the same direction. We imagine our own root guru in the form of the primordial Buddha, Dorjé Chang (in Tibetan) or Vajradhara (in Sanskrit). Dorjé Chang is symbolically represented as blue. Blue is supposed to be the colour of changelessness. Even if we add other shades or colours to a dark blue, it does not change. It is the colour of the sky and depicts the true nature of our mind, it is timeless, changeless, and it stands for the truth and an unlimited state of being. Dorjé Chang is holding a bell and a vajra in his hands crossed in the union mudra, which represent the union of wisdom and compassion. He is sitting on a sun and moon disc, on top of a lotus. This is what we visualise, but he is actually our own root guru in the form of Vajradhara.

All the lamas or masters of the lineage of Mahamudra are sitting one on top of the other, not really sitting on each other's heads, otherwise, they might slip and fall. A lama once taught this Guru Yoga to his student, who misunderstood and thought he should visualise himself sitting on the head of his guru. His guru happened to be bald. The next morning, he came to see his guru, completely tired, and told him: "Please do not ask me to do this again! It is impossible, I tried to sit on your head, but because it is so slippery, I have been falling down the whole night, and now I am completely exhausted." If unfortunately you were to visualise some lamas of the lineage with bald heads, you might see them fall down, which might affect your concentration.

This is just an anecdote, and I think that we do not actually "see" when we visualise. Maybe people who have reached the most advanced stages can see everything completely clearly and distinctly, but beginners like us cannot see completely clearly. It is enough to feel the presence of these people, all the enlightened beings, all the masters of the lineage, and not only of the lineage of our own tradition but all the other lineages, whatever they may be, throughout space, throughout the universe, all of them. We should feel that they are there, feel their benevolence, their trustworthiness and willingness to help.

As I explained before, devotion is the very positive, warm, trusting feeling we develop towards a really good friend whose sole concern and motivation is our own good, and who has the capacity to help and benefit us.

Here we are surrounded by enlightened beings, completely good, with no selfish motives, only wanting to help all sentient beings. Moreover, they not only have the willingness to help but the power to do so, therefore, we feel protected, loved, cared for. That feeling is the most important. When we have developed it, we have completed the purpose of this visualisation.

It is similar to that of the Refuge Tree we talked about before, with not just the guru, but also the Yidams, Buddhas, Dharma, all the Dakinis and Dharma protectors. However, the main focus here is on the guru.

Questions

Last time, someone asked whether we could have several gurus at the same time. Is this the reason why we visualise our guru as Dorjé Chang, I mean because he's the embodiment of all our gurus?

I think it is not the main reason why we visualise Dorjé Chang here. If you have several gurus, you can do whatever Guru Yoga and think that the main figure embodies all of them. Dorjé Chang is mainly the symbolic form of the inner guru. Dorjé Chang is what we call the "primordial Buddha", or first Buddha, which means somebody who has never been deluded, who has been enlightened for all eternity. From the Buddhist point of view, our true nature has never been deluded, it is like the sun above the clouds. What is deluded is below the clouds. That unlimited enlightened state of ourselves is Dorjé Chang, the primordial Buddha. He is a symbol of our completely enlightened nature. That is the main reason. Anyway, whether you have one or many gurus does not matter that much in this practice, it is not the point. The point here is to work with our own devotion, our own inner guru, the introduction to or the recognition and actualisation of our inner guru. How to see or "be" our inner guru is the main purpose. Although I said before that it was all right to have more than one guru, it does not mean that we should always have more than one. One good guru is enough.

How do we look at this visualisation? Do we see it as exterior to ourselves or do we identify with it?

This is just the beginning. You have already become this beautiful red dancing girl. Now in front of you is your guru, the main guru in the form of blue Dorjé Chang. You can feel this enlightened energy, really perfect unlimited compassion and wisdom. It is something you can trust, that has the capacity and the willingness to help you and everybody else, but for the moment, you are not becoming that yet. There are also exercises to actually become like that, to merge and become inseparable with it. You will eventually, maybe, when you come to the end of the practice, but for the moment you are just there looking at it, as if it were a nice dish. Ha! Ha! The better you can see it, the better you understand it, the more you will eventually be able to become like it.

I've read somewhere that the primordial Buddha is Samantabhadra. Here you say it is Vajradhara. Are they the same? Does it depend on different traditions?

You take Samantabhadra, and if you put some more ornaments on him, you have Vajradhara. They are just different iconographic forms and they can be classified into three main categories: the Dharmakaya form, the Sambhogakaya form and the Nirmanakaya form, On top of this, to make it even more complicated, there is the Dharmakaya Dharmakaya form, and the Dharmakaya Sambhogakaya form an also the Dharmakaya Nirmanakaya form. Then there are : the Sambhogakaya Dharmakaya form, the Sambhogakaya Sambhogakaya form, and the Sambhogakaya Nirmanakaya form, and so on. Samantabhadra is a Dharmakaya Dharmakaya form whereas Vajradhara is a Sambhogakaya Dharmakaya form.

We now come to a prayer which is very profound but maybe difficult to explain:

> *Om, all pervading ones, you are the very nature of all things, like space*
> *you have neither abiding or going, nor any of the material characteristics of*
> *coming or going, yet like the moon reflecting in water, you manifest wherever*
> *someone thinks of you. Glorious Herukas who conquer the armies of*
> *negative forces, gurus, yidams, dakinis and all those who accompany you, if*
> *now I pray to you with faith, please manifest here clearly the power of your*
> *non conceptual compassion.*

What is described here is the nature of the enlightened beings. Actually, it is not only enlightened beings; everything is like this, like space. It is also the theme of the Mahamudra teachings, but I will not go into that here.

Then we come to what is called the "Seven Branches Prayer". It is an exercise, a practice we do in order to work on ourselves. These seven branches are: prostrations, offerings, purification, rejoicing, requesting the teachings, requesting the benevolent great beings to live long, and dedication. This prayer is written here in a short form, but while reciting it, we can think of it in a more elaborate way.

Prostrations are a means of showing respect, by falling on our knees and stretching our body on the ground. It is a way of working on our pride. Pride is one of our negative emotions. If we have too much pride, we cannot improve, we cannot open up. It is said that trying to give something to a proud man is like pouring water on a bowl turned upside down. Nothing goes inside it.

Offerings work on our stinginess, our clinging, not being able to give or share. We start in our imagination, we create the best things we can think of and offer them to the four objects of offerings. These are; first of all, the Buddhas and Bodhisattvas and great beings who are worthy of our offering. Secondly, all sentient beings who, as the object of our compassion, are also worthy of offerings. Thirdly, all kinds of beings who have harmed us, wish to harm us, or whom we have harmed. And finally, to the beings who protect us, who benefit us, we give offerings as a sign of gratefulness. Besides visualising offerings, we also offer them praises.

Purification: we then purify all the negative things we have done in the past, are doing in the present or might be doing in the future. We repent, realising how negative and harmful they are, and take the resolution not to do them again. Purification does not mean we have to think of each negative action one by one, but rather in a general way.

Rejoicing at the good deeds others achieved is a means to work on our jealousy. We do not feel diminished because somebody else got something better or succeeded better than we did. On the contrary, we feel joyful at the success of others. If we can do this, we will never have reasons to feel unhappy, because even if we have no personal reason to rejoice, we can always find joy in the success of others. This is a very important thing.

Requesting the enlightened beings to give us teachings and to live long is also rejoicing in a way, because it means we appreciate the positive, the attainment, the wisdom and compassion of great beings, so that we wish for the good things to be shared, and for the enlightened beings to live long and remain among us.

From the Buddhist and especially from the Mahayana Buddhist point of view, dedication is regarded as one of the most important practices. It is believed that if we do something that is very positive but do not dedicate it for a big purpose, the result will certainly come, but will be short-lived. We can compare it to getting a large sum of money and going to the supermarket to buy everything. When we have spent it all, we have nothing left. On the other hand, if we dedicate even a small positive action to a great cause, the result will not be exhausted until the goal for which we have dedicated it is accomplished. Therefore the deeper, wider, bigger purpose or cause for which we dedicate, the better, larger, grander positive effects we will get. If we dedicate even a small positive deed to the enlightenment of all sentient beings, its results will be felt until it happens, we will keep on reaping the positive results. Therefore, it is like putting the whole sum on a fixed deposit in a bank, and getting a very high interest rate. These are the seven branches of the prayer.

After this comes a long prayer enumerating the names of all the holders of the lineage, right from the time of Vajradhara, with whom the lineage of the Mahamudra started. This is a very inspiring prayer, if we know the lives of these masters, otherwise it does not make much sense. I am not going to go through this, but I would advise those of you who wish to do this Guru Yoga to read the biographies of these great masters, the songs and writings they may have left behind, and the stories related to their lives, so that you understand who they were and feel inspired while reading the prayer. The more we know about these masters, the more we will develop devotion, and the better we will understand the practice, because the more we understand the experiences of the masters who have actually practised and got real experience out of it, the more we understand what the practice is about. All the names listed here are meant to make us so strongly inspired that, as is said in the texts: "all our hairs stand on end, and tears well up in our eyes". Feeling inspired is what this prayer is all about.

This reminds me of a story. A highwayman, a kind of bandit from Kham was dying. A Lama came by his side and instructed him to think of the Buddhas, the Lamas and so on. The dying Khampa answered he could not think of them. "What can you think of?" asked the Lama. "Well", answered the man, "all I can think of is this, sausages, sizzling on hot ashes, very hot, a little bursting, looking delicious." The Lama then told him: "Actually, the pure land of Dewachen is full of such hot sizzling ash-coloured sausages. They are hanging from every branch of every tree, and you do not even have to pick them up: if you lie down under a tree, they will fall in your open mouth! Even Amitabha Buddha, the main Buddha of this pure land, is also a little bit ash-coloured. Can you now think of that?" "Oh, yes, yes!" answered the highwayman. He then thought of this pure land, felt very inspired, died peacefully and was reborn in Dewachen. So if all you can think of are sizzling sausages, you can still imagine all the Lamas of the lineage holding sizzling sausages! .... But maybe you would prefer sizzling potatoes, French fries!

After the long lineage prayer there is another prayer to the lineage in a shorter form, which is also very meaningful. It is often used as an instruction for the Mahamudra. One can get a complete Mahamudra teaching on this lineage prayer alone.

The "Manam shikor", or four lines prayer, comes after the short lineage prayer. It is repeated as much as possible. It says:

All beings my mothers, throughout space, pray to the Lama, the precious Buddha,

It is not a command but an instruction, an invitation. We are not alone, we think we are surrounded by all the other beings, who are as close to us as our mother (if our mother is close to us - otherwise anybody who is close to us), and we all pray together to the Guru, whom we see as a precious Buddha.

> *All beings, my mothers, throughout space, pray to the guru,*
> *the all-pervading Dharmakaya,*

> *All beings, my mothers throughout space, pray to the guru,*
> *the very blissful Sambhogakaya,*

> *All beings, my mothers throughout space, pray to the guru,*
> *the very compassionate Nirmanakaya.*

We think of the guru as three kayas or three aspects, three forms of an enlightened being: the Dharmakaya, the Sambhogakaya and the Nirmanakaya. The Dharmakaya is the enlightened state of an enlightened being, of a Buddha's mind: completely limitless wisdom and compassion. The Dharmakaya is the aspect of limitless awareness without concepts and duality.

The Sambhogakaya is sometimes called the enjoyment body, or the blissful body. This is a Buddha's own experience of the enlightened state, how an enlightened being feels. It is an ever joyful compassionate aspect.

The Nirmanakaya is the manifestation. Wherever there is a possibility of helping anybody, wherever he is needed, a Buddha appears under whatever form is appropriate. That power to manifest spontaneously is the Nirmanakaya aspect.

A completely enlightened being is the embodiment of these three kayas. It is very difficult to describe an enlightened being, because our mind cannot conceive it in its totality. Describing a Buddha through his Kayas is an attempt to approach this other dimension through three or sometimes four aspects, this fourth kaya representing the inseparability of the three others.

Here we pray to the guru seen as inseparable from these three aspects. Whether our own guru is completely enlightened or not does not matter. Here again, what is essential is to feel devotion.

The prayer is followed by the recitation of the mantra: *Karmapa Chenno* and we repeat this as much as possible. We also repeat the following wishing prayer:

> *I pray to the precious guru,*
> *Grant your blessing that my mind may let go of the belief in a self,*
> *Grant your blessing that desirelessness be born in me,*
> *Grant your blessing that non Dharma thoughts may cease,*
> *Grant your blessing that I may realise my mind as unborn,*
> *Grant your blessing that delusion may subside of itself,*
> *Grant your blessing that phenomena be realised to be the Dharmakaya*

We pray like this for ourselves and for all sentient beings. We never do this Guru Yoga or any Vajrayana practice for ourselves alone, we always think that all other sentient beings throughout space are present around us, and we do our practice together with them.

The prayer "*Calling the lama from afar*" comes next. It is quite long and whether we do it completely or select several passages will depend on the time we can devote to our practice.

At the end, we have the empowerments. This is a very important part which we cannot leave out. We find empowerments in all Guru Yoga practices. First we say a prayer to request the empowerments:

> *Glorious perfect guru, please grant me the four empowerments that bring*
> *spiritual maturity. Bless me that I may quickly be ripe for the four streams*
> *of practice. Grant me accomplishment of the four activities.*

After we have said this prayer, those who accompany the main figure, all the gurus of the lineage and all the enlightened beings disappear, melt into light and merge with the main guru in the centre, Vajradhara, who represents our own guru and thus becomes the embodiment of all the Precious Ones. The text says:

Then from him, a white light emanates from his forehead and dissolves in my forehead, it purifies all obstructions caused by physical misdeeds, I receive the vase empowerment, enabling me to practise the visualisation stage of meditation, I now have the fortunate opportunity of achieving the Nirmanakaya.

From his throat, a read light emanates and dissolves into my throat, and dissolves all obscurations caused by speech, I receive the secret empowerment enabling me to meditate on the subtle channels and energies. I now have the fortunate opportunity of achieving the Sambhogakaya.

From his heart, a blue light emanates and dissolves into my heart, and purifies all obstructions of the mind. I receive the wisdom empowerment, enabling me to practise the meditation that establishes the stability. I now have the fortunate opportunity of achieving the Dharmakaya.

Then the three lights, white, red and blue radiate together and purify simultaneously my three centres. I receive the fourth empowerment enabling me to realise Mahamudra. I now have the fortunate possibility of achieving the Svabhavikakaya, the union of the three kayas.

We now feel that we have completely, experientially realised the enlightened state of Mahamudra. This is what we call the Four Empowerments of body, speech, mind, and all three together. When we receive it, we should very strongly feel that we are transformed, that we actualise the enlightened state. This is a very important part and almost the end of the Guru Yoga.

After having given the empowerments, the guru melts, becomes a ball of light, and that ball of light enters into our body through the top of our head, and we become one with him:

> *The guru's three vajras, (that is his body, mind and speech) are*
> *undifferentiated and of one taste, endowed with the three-fold mindfulness*
> *that integrates everything into the path, spontaneous presence, quality and*
> *automatic liberation*

This is a literal translation. It means that we become one with the guru, one with the enlightened state. Our mind and the guru's mind, the enlightened beings mind become one. Our inner guru has been awakened. We are one, there is no difference between the enlightened beings and ourselves.

We try to "*be*" in that state of mind, to remain in that meditation, and that is the end of the Guru Yoga.

We have come to the conclusion and there is no separation between our outer and inner guru. We see our true nature, which is actually the Buddha. In that unlimited, non conceptual state of being, we remain for some time and rest in a relaxed way. Relaxation is important at every stage of practice in Buddhism. We cannot practise with tensions. Although we have to be very diligent, we have to practise in a very subtle, relaxed way. The more relaxed we are, the more spacious we become and the better our practice will be. If we practice in a forceful way, being too tight, too tense, we can encounter some problems, therefore it is advised to relax.

At the end comes a long version of the dedication prayer:

> *Every being without exception has the vajra mind, eternal and blissful.*
> *I dedicate the virtue generated by this practice to them all since it brings*
> *Buddhahood, immortality, through the union of skills and understanding and*
> *entry into changelessness through the inner path.*

Through this virtue may I quickly achieve the Mahamudra and thereafter may I bring all beings, without exception, to that same state.

Through the blessings of the Buddha's achievement of the three kayas, through the blessing of the truth of the changeless Dharma and through the blessing of the Sangha's undivided aspiration, may this dedication prayer come true.

Through the goodness of all the roots of virtue I have gathered in the three times, may I, in all my lives, collect and uphold the pure teachings of my Guru, Karmapa, the Lord of Dharma. Thereby may the development of my own and others' understanding be brought to complete maturity.

May I, in each and every one of my existences, be like splendid Vajrapani, unerring in everything related to the quintessence of the subtle form, speech and mind.

May I always be a fitting vessel for the study of, and realisation through insight of all aspects of liberation of the subtle form, speech and mind.

May I never be separate from them in all my existences, even for an instant, just as the body is never separate from its shadow.

May I achieve the felicity of the five joys.

May I be able to complete all my projects, just as planned, through learning a vast panorama of activities which cultivate the two accumulations.

May I never be lazy even for a moment in being an instrument of my guru's activity.

May I achieve his works through the four modes of peaceful, increasing, powerful and wrathful activity.

May whatever actions I perform through my three doors carry my Guru's instructions to completion.

May what I achieve through the nine modes of service be pleasing to him.

May whatever virtuous, unvirtuous or neutral action I perform be something which is pleasing to him.

May I never for an instant do something which is displeasing to him.

May I be the instrument of the principal activity of my Guru and great master of Dharma.

May I become the inheritor of the teachings of my Guru.

May I become able to quell all sickness, strife and famine throughout the ten directions.

May I truly actualise the Mahamudra at the clear light stage of death.

May there be no intermediate bardo manifestations but integration into the mandala of glorious Vajrasattva. Abiding in that state, may I elevate all beings to the state of great Vajradhara through the mighty play of the Vajrayana.

In brief, may I become like my Guru, the profound master of Dharma, one through whom there is liberation when seen, when heard, when called to mind and when touched.

May I ever be mindful, in the depth of my heart, of the absolute certainty in death.

May I enter the blessing of Mikyo Gawa through complete authentic renunciation born of total weariness with Samsara and the growth of natural faith and devotion.

May there never be, either for myself or any other person, involvement with arrogance about oneself, condemnation of others and delight in others' weaknesses and downfalls.

In all my existences, may I be nurtured and cared for by the best of all friends, the supremely caring holder of the Black Crown, the essence of yidams, glorious Dewacho and Korlo Dompa.

May I, in each and every one of my existences, achieve the state never separate from guru Mikyo Dorjé, yidam Dorjé Naljorma, Dharma protector Bernachen and so forth.

Every being, without exception, has the Vajra mind, eternal and blissful. I dedicate the virtue (generated by this practice) to them, since it brings Buddhahood - immortality, through the union of skills and understanding, and entry into changelessness through the inner path.

This dedication ends the practice of Guru Yoga.

Sö nam di yi tam che sik pa nyi
Top ne nye pay dra nam pam je ne
Kye ga na chi ba lap truk pa yi
Si pay tso le dro wa drol war shok

Through the wholesomeness of this practice
May all mental defilements be overcome
And may all beings be liberated from the ocean of samsara,
Stirred by the waves of ageing, sickness, birth and death.

All my babbling
In the name of Dharma
Has been set down faithfully
By my dear students of pure vision.

I pray that at least a fraction of the wisdom
Of those enlightened teachers
Who tirelessly trained me
Shine through this mass of incoherence.

May the sincere efforts of all those
Who have worked tirelessly
Result in spreading the true meaning of Dharma
To all who aspire to know.

May this also help to dispel the darkness of ignorance
In the minds of all living beings
And lead them to complete realisation
Free from all fear.

(As desired this dedication was written by Ringu Tulku, 8th of July, 1997, Dublin)